An excellent book...   *...New Haven Sunday Register*

If you've ever thought of putting your story into book form...be sure to look into Denis Ledoux's *Turning Memories Into Memoirs.*   *...The VVA Veteran*

TMIM deserves your attention before you begin your story.
...Jacksonville Times-Union

Ledoux's book will be immediately useful for anyone about to embark on writing personal history.   *...Maine Sunday Telegram*

Ledoux makes big promises... and he achieves them. *...Portsmouth [NH] Herald*

Very beneficial...helps writers get off to a great start.   *...A.L.A. Booklist*

TMIM is lively, entertaining, and practical...   *...Yankee Magazine*

TMIM is a guide that brings one's past alive and helps one to share it with others in a way that will capture interest.   *...Wisconsin Bookwatch*

[Writing memoirs may be] the next best thing to reliving life. *...New York Times*

Anyone intent on writing a family history should read *TMIM....Baltimore Sun*

A satisfying way to preserve experience and pass along information to another generation.   *...Christian Science Monitor*

TMIM helps solve your problem of what to give an older adult for Christmas.
...The Cincinnati Post

Contains countless helpful suggestions...   *...DownEast Magazine*

A step-by-step manual to writing successful memoirs, even for those who think they don't know how.   *...West Hawaii Today*

Fun to read, filled with practical tips and stimulating ideas.
...Quincy [MA] Patriot-Ledger

COPYRIGHT: C. 1993 BY DENIS LEDOUX

ALL RIGHTS RESERVED. No part of this book may be used or reproduced in any manner whatsoever without the written permission of the author except in the case of brief quotations.

PRINTED IN THE USA
FIRST EDITION, FOURTH PRINTING

SOLEIL PRESS ✪ 95 GOULD ROAD #12, LISBON FALLS, MAINE 04252

PUBLISHER'S CATALOGUING IN PUBLICATION DATA
Ledoux, Denis, 1947-
    Turning Memories Into Memoirs / A Handbook for Writing Lifestories
    1. Creative writing.– 2. Self actualization (psychology).– 3. Autobiography.
    I. Title
    ISBN 0-9619373-2-7

BOOK & COVER DESIGN: Martha Blowen

On the cover: Pat Chaffers Croteau's grand-parents, Magloire Bolduc & Marie Gagné Bolduc, with their daughter, Berthe, c. 1903. All photos otherwise unidentified in this book are from Ledoux and Blowen family collections.

Acknowledgements: ↣ Original development of the **Turning Memories into Memoirs** workshops was made possible in part by grants from the Maine Humanities Council. ↣ Mary Walsh of the Foster Grandparents Program of the Maine Bureau of the Elderly and Adult Services, and Peter Haggerman gave generously of their time and energy to realize the initial series. ↣ Arthur Whitman, a former TMIM workshopper, and John Clobridge of the Amherst,(MA) Senior Center, both read and responded to this manuscript in early versions– many thanks. ↣ Soleil Press is indebted to its '91-'92 interns Ami Berger & Jessica Sheridan of Bates , Rob Christie of Bowdoin, and especially to Stephanie Doyon of Colby and Lisbon, Maine, for the many hours they contributed to our projects and to this book: *merci beaucoup!* ↣ Simone Martell of Bates and Gwen Thompson of Bowdoin ('92-'93 interns) helped make the first printing a success: thanks. ↣ It's hard to say which was most valuable-- your insightful editing or your timely enthusiasm– Ellen Laflèche, we thank you, thank you! ↣ Ladora Davis Blowen, who appears in several of our treasured photos, is a treasure herself & helped once again in more ways than we can say. ↣ Maxim, your patience in the last weeks of editing and producing this book deserve to go into your lifestory someday. Thanks: you're our hero! ↣ Paula Everett, Laurette Gagné, and the others at Horizon 55 in Lewiston, Janet Foley at 55+ in Brunswick, Dorothy Elwell at Senior Spectrum in Belfast, and Harriet Mosher at the Maine Writers and Publishers Alliance in Brunswick have steadfastly made the workshops available to their clients: thank you all! ↣

TURNING MEMORIES
INTO
Memoirs
a Handbook for Writing Lifestories

Denis Ledoux

Soleil ✹ Press

For my mémère, Marie Bilodeau Ledoux

When I was a child, she told me stories that have stayed with me all my life.

For all those, too, who have turned, and will turn, their memories into memoirs.

By the same author

Short Fiction

What Became and Them and Other Stories From Franco-America
Mountain Dance and Other Stories

Anthology

Lives in Translation: An Anthology of Contemporary
Franco-American Writings

Bibliography

Bibliography of Franco-American Works

Table of Contents

Introduction

There is power in storytelling, and it is accessible to you. *Turning Memories Into Memoirs* will initiate you into the process of writing your personal and family lifestories. This book will help you to make decisions on *what* to write as well as on *how* and *why* to write your stories. Soon you will find yourself working the magic of lifewriting for yourself and for your family.

This book has evolved from my work in the last four years. I have guided people in the process of remembering and writing down their stories through workshops and through editing individual manuscripts.

One day in 1988, I read from my first collection of short stories° to a group of Foster Grandparent volunteers. Several dozen men and women, sitting at long tables, many smiling in agreement with the stories I had just shared, said, in one way or another, "These are people just like us!" They seemed to recognize the child climbing the apple tree at the edge of the meadow or to see once again their own parents in the tired women and men trudging through the tenement district on their way back from the textile factory.

After I read *my* stories that day, my listeners began to tell me *theirs*. These were set in a number of countries around the world and in a variety of cultures within this country. As people spoke, some grew animated while others exuded great peace. Some spoke with pride; others, with sorrow. All, however, seemed to *need* to tell the stories of their lives and of their families.

Once again, storytelling-- in this case, from my fam-

"The telling of your stories is a revolutionary act."
- Sam Keen
author

"My life might seem ordinary to others, but it wasn't to me. I made a good life for myself."
- Workshop writer

° *What Became of Them and Other Stories from Franco-America*, Soleil Press, 1988.

ily's fictionalized past-- had "primed the pump" of memory to enable personal and family stories to pour out. After my reading that day, I went home feeling justified in my faith in the primal function of storytelling. It affirms, and reaffirms, meaning in our lives.

"Those were terrible days. I survived both Stalin and Hitler. My children need to know what it was like to live in a time when devils were on the earth."
- Workshop writer

After I had read from my collection of stories to a second group of Foster Grandparent volunteers, the state director of the program reached me at home. "My volunteers would like to write their lifestories," she said. "Would you be available to help them?"

"Yes!" was my immediate response to this opportunity to help people gain access to the power of their lifestories. The proposal she and I wrote for a lifewriting project eventually received two major grants from the Maine Humanities Council.

This book is based on the success of those workshops and the many sessions I have presented in the years since.

Don't lose your stories!

Your stories-- the one about the time you woke up in the night to see flames shooting out of the barn or about the cross-country trip your family took to look for work during the Depression years or about how your grandparents met in Lithuania-- these are the stories that have shaped you and your family.

"I always thought that if I couldn't write like a pro I shouldn't write at all. With that kind of thinking, you end up with nothing!"
- Workshop writer

We might even say that **we *are* the stories we tell; we are the stories that members of our family tell *about themselves* and *about us*.**

You intend to record your personal and family stories, of course-- someday. For now, though, you tell yourself, writing these stories will have to wait. There are so many of them. Where do you start? Where do you go from there? And you're busy-- you know how it is! You don't have the time to figure out how to go about writing and organizing your stories. You tell yourself you're better off relegating the task to another time-- or to another person.

Remember how your uncle, or perhaps it was your aunt, told marvelous stories about your people back in

Canada-- or was it Sweden? But now the family storyteller is gone and where are the stories? Gone too? Lost? Not just the general information ("Our family came from the city of Bratislava in Slovakia") but the details of history and humor, of success and disappointment that flesh out a story and make it real ("When we would get up in the morning in the wintertime in those unheated upstairs bedrooms, my brother Bob and I could see our breaths frozen in the cold air"). Many of these details that explain so much about how you and your family were shaped are lost because the family storyteller didn't have the time to write them down-- or perhaps was intimidated by the idea of writing.

And you, all these years, you've been a housewife, or an insurance agent, or a mill worker, or a math teacher. You haven't done much writing-- and high school or college English class was so long ago. How can anyone expect *you* to write your stories!

"If you start well, you will write all your stories."
- Natalie Goldberg
poet

Write your stories-- now!

This book will lead you through a step-by-step process that will enable you to produce your personal and family stories-- one at a time, one after another. In the *Turning Memories Into Memoirs* workshops, hundreds of people-- "just like you"-- have written thousands of pages of memoirs for themselves and for their families. Even those who insisted they couldn't write and declared they had never written anything before the workshop, have composed dozens, sometimes hundreds, of pages-- and the pages have added up to coherent, interesting, and rewarding lifestories.

With the help of *Turning Memories Into Memoirs*, writing your stories won't be as hard as you may think.

✐ *Turning Memories Into Memoirs* will **increase your ability to remember** more vividly the **details** of the stories you want to tell.

✐ *Turning Memories Into Memoirs* will offer **concrete suggestions** for fleshing out your writing with **proven sto-**

Like all long-term projects, lifewriting will have its ups and downs. If you experience a down, keep in mind that what you are undertaking is wonderful and important and the rewards to you and your family will be great!

rytelling techniques. Ultimately, of course, *it's not enough to remember* your story-- you must *tell* it in an interesting and meaningful way both for yourself and for your reader.

"I remember him as uncaring, but he paid my college tuition. I had forgotten that. Why?"
- Workshop writer

✎ *Turning Memories Into Memoirs* will teach you the skills to **gain access to your life's deeper, inner meaning**-- to the realm of your spirit. Using these simple writing techniques, it will be possible for you to achieve a new understanding, a new appreciation, of the inner, psychological aspects of your life and of your family history.

How to read this book

✎ **First, read the two initial chapters**. They will create the context from which to understand what follows.

✎ **Then, either read the rest of the book in the order presented or flip through it** to sections that seem to be the most helpful to you at your stage of writing. In the *Turning Memories Into Memoirs* workshops, I generally present material in the order set in these pages. However, individuals will often ask for specific help or information-- and we deal with those questions as they arise, not when they were scheduled to be presented.

You can approach this book in the same way. Familiarize yourself with the table of contents and read those chapters first which will help you the most.

There is ample blank space in the margins. Use it to make notes or to write your own marginal quotes. This is your book! Make it work for you!

It's ok to start with the writing skills you have now. As you write, you will learn more about writing and your skills will increase.

✎ **Read the lifestories which follow each chapter** and those gathered together in Appendix A. These are stories written by people "just like you"-- people who one day decided to write their lifestories and then proceeded to do it.

These writers stood at the place where you now stand, at the beginning of a rewarding exploration of their personal and family pasts or perhaps at the threshold of a new stage of self-growth.

Let these stories be your support and encouragement: **you too will succeed in writing your lifestories.**

Tools you'll need in lifewriting

You probably have everything you'll need at home to write your lifestories. Here's what I recommend you use:

✔ **a three-ring loose-leaf binder**. This sort of notebook allows you to add to your collection of stories at any time or to take text away from it. A bound notebook is much less flexible. With a ring binder, you can easily add text without worrying if the next pages are already filled in. It is also easy to remove sections without ripping anything out or making ugly slash marks.

✔ **manila folders**. These will be useful to keep discarded stories and story fragments which you might want to recycle into your text later. They will also be handy to fill up with interview and research notes.

✔ **a typewriter or a computer word processor**. Some people write their finished stories by hand. This is certainly a possibility, but a typed or printed version is much easier to read. See Chapter 7, Section I, for more on this topic.

Chapter 1   Before You Start

A.   Tell me a story!

B.   You, too, can be a storyteller.

C.   What moves you to write your stories?

D.   The payoff: what's in it for you?

E.   Scope: what's right for you?

F.   Make a schedule for success.

Lifestories from the Workshops:

Sophia's Masterpiece *by Leonore Burke*

An Introduction to Education *by Leland Davis*

Leonore Lazuk Burke, c. 1948

A. Tell me a story!

Stories fascinate us all our lives. As children, we loved to be told fairy tales and to hear, time after time, the tales our parents told us about what we did and said when we were babies, and about their own childhoods. As soon as we were old enough, we told stories about ourselves for our parents and for our friends.

As adults, we speak in stories at work, at family get-togethers, at class reunions, at town meetings, at the post office when we meet our neighbors. In fact, stories are such an important medium for us that even the numerous stories we tell and hear are not enough to satisfy our enormous appetites-- we consume additional stories reading novels, seeing movies, and watching dramas on television.

What is the meaning behind telling (and listening to) all of these stories? Obviously, stories *entertain* us, but our need to be entertained doesn't fully account for our great hunger for stories. A more satisfying explanation of the power stories hold for us is that they provide *rehearsals* for life: they furnish us with the *reassurance* and the *guidance* we need to become adults and live full and happy lives.

Let's see if this idea holds true when we examine a story we all know: Hansel and Gretel. In this story, the children are abandoned by a wicked stepmother and a weak-willed father. The children rescue themselves by killing the witch. In the end, in spite of his initial lapse, their "true" parent (the reformed father) welcomes them back and promises to protect them against overpowering adult forces (the stepmother and the father's own weaker side).

Does this story provide reassurance and guidance? It

Think of this chapter as a warm up. Before you can start writing your lifestory, you must understand the context out of which you will be writing. This chapter will help you to feel confident and comfortable about telling your stories.

"I needed to live, but I also needed to record what I lived."
- Anaïs Nin
diarist

certainly does. The story reassures children that there is always hope of a happy ending no matter how bad things get and that their true parents do love them in spite of their weaknesses. It also tells children that, although they themselves are weak and vulnerable, they are capable of working out solutions to help themselves. It is Gretel, after all, who pushes the witch into the oven.

We can learn a lot about people by the stories they tell. For instance, Edith is always the butt of her own jokes, while Tony never tells a story that doesn't illustrate how cleverly he got the better of some unwitting adversary.

Grown-ups tell stories and listen eagerly to others tell theirs for the same reasons. We, too, are looking for order and meaning in the chaos of our lives. When we say, "After the house burned down, she went to pieces. She forgot she had a family to live for", we are telling a story that contains reassurance and guidance about order. We are saying that, in spite of the calamity, this woman could have found comfort and meaning in her relationships. It is a clear message to both the listener and the speaker: tragedies can either be compounded or overcome-- it's up to us to choose.

We read novels or watch movies for the same reason we tell stories: we want to be reassured that we can succeed in this struggle called life. We want to see and hear how others have done this in their lives. What meaning is there to their decisions: did finishing school afford them a better job? was putting off marriage a sensible thing to do? what were the consequences of following or deviating from the patterns their families had set for them?

A lifestory is a gift one generation bestows upon another, a legacy people have been giving from the beginning of time.

We want stories to reassure us that the inner strength we can manage to muster will be sufficient against self-doubt, loss, grief, and disappointment. (People often exaggerate in their stories not to aggrandize themselves or to boast, but to *rehearse* the strength and meaning that may be missing in their lives and, by doing that, to acquire the strength and meaning they need.)

It's not out of idle curiosity that your children and grandchildren want to know about you and your life. What is more natural than for them to turn to the stories of their own parents and family for reassurance and guidance? Your stories have this power and, if they are preserved, they can offer meaning and direction for your children and grandchildren-- just as they can for you.

"How can the arts overcome the slow dying of men's hearts that we call progress?"
- W.B. Yeats
poet

When you tell your personal and family stories, you are filling a need that exists not only in your family but in the life of the larger human community to receive guidance and reassurance. Every year, as more and more once-tightly-knit groups in our society unravel and our access to our rightful inheritance of family stories is threatened, telling your stories becomes increasingly more important.

Exercise

✔ Recall (in your mind or in conversation) a family story you heard when you were a child. This story may be a fragment-- in fact, that's how most family stories are handed down.

✔ Now, write a list of the details you remember about the story (or fragment). At this stage, you are not writing narrative, just making a list. The following might be included: the names of the people in the story; their relationships to each other and to you; what they did for pleasure and work; what the story's context was (physically-- the place and event; spiritually-- the ideas and emotions; culturally-- the attitudes and the ways of doing things); what the conflict (the action that leads to a crisis) was; and how it was resolved.

✔ Use short sentences, phrases, or even just single words. Don't try to write text.

✔ Be as specific as you can with the details ("auburn hair braided into a coil"; "a scar from beneath his left nostril to just under his left ear lobe"). Try to remember what people might have worn (high lace collar dresses), or how they might have spoken ("it was as dark as the inside of a pocket"), etc.

✔ Using this list (which should considerably stimulate your memory), now write a rough first draft of the story. Since writing is a different medium from speaking, you may feel yourself less fluent in writing than in speaking the story. Don't let this bother you. It is a natural reaction, and the practice of writing will change this.

✔ Reread your rough draft-- not for how well you have written this story but for what it tells you about the nature and the role of storytelling. What qualities (usually something like: courage, faith, love) speak to something so deep in you that you are still moved by them after all these years? These provide what I have called either *guidance* or *reassurance*.

✔ Keep this story draft in your loose-leaf binder as a working copy. Later you will learn to expand and improve it. **Use this list-making method to create rough drafts of many stories as they occur to you.**

B. You, too, can be a storyteller.

This section focuses on a few crucial factors that make a story successful.

"The least thing done with meaning is worth more in life than the greatest of things without it."
- C.G. Jung
psychologist

Some people come to lifewriting with a natural facility for storytelling. Don't despair if you aren't one of them. To a great extent, this is a facility which can be learned. It's a matter of acquiring both *technical skills* and *belief* in yourself and in your role as storyteller.

1) **You can learn to make effective use of a variety of technical skills to write successful stories.** I will mention only a few here, but in other sections of this book you will learn many more.

✐ Successful stories usually have a recognizable *beginning* ("It was the year I was three that my father fell sick"); a *middle* that tells what happened in the story ("He took to bed; my mother went to work; I lived with my grandmother"); and an *end* that reveals how the story concludes ("He died, and we began to piece our lives together again").

✐ Successful stories have *characters* who are recognizably human beings. This is important: even if you are writing about someone you do not like and you want to show only their faults, you should write about some positive qualities or habits in that person. Otherwise, your readers will not feel the humanity of the character and may not only dismiss what you say about *that* person but also whatever it is you want your whole story to convey (see Chapter 5, Section D).

✐ Successful stories have *conflicts* (the clash of opposing or contradictory desires or unfolding of events-- "We wanted my father to live and did everything we could for him; his body was exhausted though, and he lost his will to fight") that are resolved before the end (see Chapter

Chapter 3, Section A).

✐ Successful stories are full of *sensual details* (colors, shapes, textures, smells, sounds, flavors-- see Chapter 3, Section A). When your stories portray a sensual world (*three sweet-scented roses*) rather than a vague one (*some nice flowers*), you make it easier for us readers to take the leap of faith into the world of your writing.

If your story has abstract and vague wording like "After a while absence from home made fidelity difficult for him and he committed adultery...", your readers will be less interested in (and less swayed by) what you have to say than if your narration is filled with concrete and sensual details such as "One evening, in his fourth month away from his wife, he went into a bar. He had worked in the sun all day building houses and he was very tired. Somebody played a love song on the jukebox. He met a waitress with piercing black eyes. He told her a story and her laughter rang in his ears. He had not talked to a woman in this way since he had left home and..."

The Greek myth of the Labyrinth illustrates this need for sensual and material details in stories. The Labyrinth was a maze of passageways at the center of which lived a monster. In the story, a young man, Theseus, entered the Labyrinth to slay the Minotaur (half man/half bull). Many young men had entered the Labyrinth before him only to become lost in the maze. Theseus had the *sense* to connect himself to the outside world by a material detail: he used a string. After slaying the Minotaur, he was able to follow his string and retrace his steps out of the Labyrinth to re-enter the outside world.

The wonderful thing about the Labyrinth story is how it provides not only entertainment but *guidance* and *reassurance* for us as lifewriters. Lifewriters enter a literary maze at the center of which is "the truth" about their lives. If we are not to get lost in the psychological and emotional labyrinth of characters and events, we and our readers must be connected to the world by sensual and material details just as Theseus needed to be connected to the outside world by a string.

2) **You can acquire belief in your role as storyteller so necessary to tell your stories effectively.** If you tell your stories as honestly as you can you will come to believe in

Your three-ring binder is a flexible tool. Because you can remove and insert material anywhere within your continuing story, it is easy to revise your text as new ideas for its content and its format occur to you. As the number of pages grows, so will your sense of accomplishment and confidence. You will see your book of lifestories materialize before your disbelieving eyes!

the rightness and importance of what you are doing. This will lend your stories a moral authority. They will transport us just as the ancient epics do.

Storytellers (and modern artists) are at their best when telling stories not just because they want to entertain with their virtuosity but because they have come to know that stories have an inherent role to play in guiding us to live our lives meaningfully and reassuring us it can be done.

"I go ... to forge in the smithy of my soul the uncreated conscience of my race."
- James Joyce
novelist

The calling to be a storyteller is priestlike. In some way, even if you don't understand or accept it now, you, too, are responding to this calling.

✏ As you do more and more lifewriting, you will not only become better with the technical skills (telling the *how* and the *what*) of writing, but you will also begin to understand and accept your role as a storyteller.

Exercise

This exercise will help you to assess your role as a storyteller.

✔ Choose a storyteller you would like to write about and recall some memorable stories s/he once told you.

✔ Make a list of the elements that made his tales memorable. Was it plot, or character development, or setting? Was the storyteller adept at the technical details: creating drama? reproducing dialogue? setting a scene? Was it the importance of the contents that interested you? (Remember that the drama of the subject itself is usually not enough. We've all known people who have bored us to tears as they narrated "exciting" elements of a divorce, lawsuit, or accident, etc.)

✔ How did the storyteller see himself as a storyteller? Was he, and the tale, memorable because of his perception: the depth of insight? his conviction or compassion? Was it his moral authority (i.e., sense of the importance of the story's message)? What relationship did the teller have to the story: was he an active participant? an observer? Was he sympathetic? engaged with his subject? humorous? How did this relationship affect the stories?

✔ How do you yourself relate to these qualities? Which ones are important to you?

✔ Did you know another storyteller whose stories were less successful? What was it that was missing, or present in the wrong proportions? (Sometimes we can learn a lot from what *doesn't* work!)

At the workshops

Tom was from the Azores. He sat in the front of the room, a dark man among paler Franco-American and Yankee faces, and he listened attentively to my presentation on lifewriting.

When I asked for comments, Tom said, "Where I come from, there are older people who tell the stories of our islands. They know all the stories-- even the ones about before people living there now were born.

"Whenever we get together, the storytellers tell these stories. While they speak, they look around to see who's listening-- especially the children. There'll be some of the kids-- most of them really-- who don't take too long to start fidgeting, you know. They want to be someplace else, anywhere else. 'Who's that by the river?' and 'What's that noise over there?' These kids leave as soon as they can.

"There's another group of children who are so-so interested and they listen a while longer, but soon they've had enough and they wander away, too. The storyteller just has more to tell than these kids want to know.

"But, then there are the others who don't walk away-- maybe just a few, one or two even. They listen to the storyteller's every word. It's as if they can't hear enough. It's not because they're being polite or because someone told them to listen. It's because they need the stories the way other children need to run and play.

"The storyteller knows there are kids like these-- probably he was one himself-- and he makes sure he tells them all his stories. He knows these kids will be the storytellers for the island when he is gone.

"Don't you have this here, too? You should tell people that all their children need to hear some of their stories and that some of their children, the ones who are really listening even if they're only one or two, these kids need to hear all the stories. Who else will give these children their stories unless you tell them?"

Tom paused a moment and then he said, "People must tell their stories. The kids need them."

C. *What moves you to write your stories?*

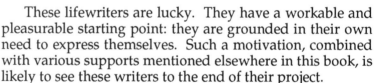

This section explores some of the motivations that lead to success in lifewriting.

Writing your lifestories will require a lot of *motivation*. The following are motivations which have inspired participants in past workshops.

1) **Many people tell a story because they derive pleasure from the telling itself.** They enjoy the unfolding of the tale, the discovery inherent in creating a story. They are enlivened by the connection with the past which telling their stories provides. These people have thoughts such as:

> *I need or want to share the pleasure I have had.*
> *I need or want to memorialize people and events of my past.*
> *I need or want to have the energy of storytelling in my life.*
> *I feel a calling to participate in something larger than myself.*

These lifewriters are lucky. They have a workable and pleasurable starting point: they are grounded in their own need to express themselves. Such a motivation, combined with various supports mentioned elsewhere in this book, is likely to see these writers to the end of their project.

2) **Some people come to recognize that they have an agenda of troubling memories to be soothed and eventually resolved.** Their untold stories seem to threaten them from deep inside, and like Theseus with the monster Minotaur, they may wish to "slay" them. These lifewriters may have such thoughts as:

> *I need or want to understand my life.*
> *I need or want to see which family patterns reveal themselves across the generations of my family.*
> *I need or want to work through some blocks I have in relation to myself and my family or my past.*

If this second set of thoughts describes your motivation

to write your personal and family stories, you are in luck: lifewriting is often a successful means of expelling personal demons. This sort of writing is often not easy; if, however, you find that telling your story frees you of anger or fear or anxiety, you will be strongly motivated to continue because, for you too, lifewriting will be grounded in *your* needs, not someone else's.

Lifewriting is often therapeutic but it is *not* therapy. Some workshop participants have found themselves overwhelmed with painful memories and have sought the help of a therapist or a support group to work with these. If you feel you can't continue alone, it may be a sign that you need the professional help of someone trained to lead you through therapy.

3) **Others approach lifewriting from a completely different perspective.** They are likely to have thoughts such as:

> *I ought to do it.*
> *It's a good thing to do.*
> *My children want me to do it, and I want to please them.*

These last reasons won't, by themselves, provide a solid foundation for a lifewriting project. They are based on meeting someone else's need instead of your own. Rather than motivate writers, these reasons are more likely to slow them down by making them feel guilty. To assuage their consciences, these writers will likely have thoughts such as these:

> *It's important work, but I'm just too busy right now!*
> *I just didn't have time this week!*
> *I really don't have anything to say!*

Ask yourself, "Is lifewriting an effort I *need to make*?" (This is not the same question as, "Is lifewriting an effort I feel *capable of making*?") If you enjoy storytelling or if lifewriting is something you must do to meet an inner need, then you will find yourself more *willing* to make the effort. Being more willing, you will commit yourself and your time to the effort needed to acquire the *capability* to succeed. Haven't you already succeeded at many difficult tasks because you were motivated to do them (perhaps it

"We are taught in our recovery from trauma not to share the stories of abuse except with appropriate support people. I need to stop working on my lifewriting project for a while to work on my issues in a survivors support group."
- Workshop writer

"This above all ask yourself in the stillest hour of the night: must I write?"
- R.M. Rilke
poet

was raising a family, nurturing a career, or supporting a parent or mate through a difficult illness)?

The task of lifewriting will not require more work and energy than you are capable of, but writing your lifestories will require some sacrifice-- especially if you haven't done much writing before.

Lifewriting is important. Believe in your stories enough to commit yourself-- today, tomorrow, and the day after.

Exercise

✔ Compile a list of the motivations you have for writing your lifestories. (e.g., "I've had an interesting life and I want to share my experience; I want to understand why I was always attracted to jobs that I would fail at.")

✔ Now write a mission statement that begins with "I am going to write my lifestories because..." Does this written statement indicate a *need to write*?

✔ This statement, which will list benefits you foresee in taking on this project, is likely to change as you pursue lifewriting and become more and more aware of its possibilities. What's important now is that your statement be heartfelt and that it reflect your motivations.

✔ Review this statement periodically and change it, or add to it, as you need to.

D. The Payoff: *what's in it for you?*

This section lists benefits you will derive from lifewriting.

As you write your lifestory, you will benefit in many ways from the experience.

1) **You will develop a record of your personal and family story.** This record will be a permanent one you can hand down to succeeding generations of your family. You will have the satisfaction of knowing that you have fulfilled your responsibility in preserving your family's past.

Your children and grandchildren will be very grateful for this written legacy.

2) **You will enjoy the sense of celebration that comes from sharing a "tale well-told".** Merely telling stories brings many people great satisfaction. Even if you have never felt it before, you will experience pleasure in celebrating your life experiences through storytelling.

3) **You will gain insights about yourself and your family.** As you view parts of your life in relation to other parts (and also begin to view it as a whole), you will undoubtedly perceive patterns and choices that facilitated or restricted growth for you or other members of your family. This may challenge the ways in which you have previously understood your life or your family. Rather than continue to insist that things are "just the way they are", you may now appreciate the help you have received or see past difficulties not as fate but as symptoms of unresolved personal or family problems.

"That a man may be free of his ghosts/ he must return to them like a garden."
- Maxine Kumin
poet

Although most of us spend no more than 20 or so years living with our families, we remain bound in various ways to family culture for the rest of our lives: what we eat, the way we use money, how we view leisure time, etc., may still be influenced by how our family taught us to deal with these matters. In addition, no matter how supportive or loving our parents may have been (and certainly not all parents are), no family on earth is perfect in its ability to nurture and cherish each individual child who comes to it. Sometimes family patterns have constricted a writer's life (e.g., views of sexuality), or unfulfilled childhood longings (e.g., to be loved for one's self) have been concealed from him by overlays of beliefs ("we love all our children equally in our family!"). Although these practices and beliefs may have hitherto remained unexamined, they have been and are powerful in their ability to limit and shape your life's possibilities.

"As you walk, you cut open and create that riverbed into which the stream of your descendants shall enter and flow."
- Nikos Kazantzakis
novelist

Your children, too, are products of your extended family and its history. The families we form with our mates can be dominated by tensions and struggles that originate from our birth families and the generations of family before us. Writing about what happened and why is one way you can break these repeating cycles of difficulty.

The task is not an easy one, but to understand your nu-

The sins of the father-- or the mother-- are visited upon the sons and daughters unto the third and fourth generations!

*We are never too old
to take a more
proactive role in our
own lives.*

*"By the creative act,
we are able to reach
beyond our own
death."*
- Rollo May
psychologist

clear and extended family cultures is often to empower yourself to be more detached from any negative hold they have on you-- whether you are 20 or 40 or 60 or 80!

Sometimes people will say, "But, shouldn't these unpleasant (or horrible) things just be forgotten? Why stir up bad memories?" The answer is clear, I think, because our families may forget the past, *but the past will not forget our families.* The "sins" of our ancestors reveal moral and spiritual traits that can run from generation to generation. Who would think it admirable for parents to hide from their children the knowledge that genetic kidney or lung or sight problems ran in a family? Clearly that is an unconscionable and foolish silence. Knowledge of such diseases may be necessary for our children to seek the care they need to compensate for or overcome inherited physical shortcomings.

On the moral or spiritual plane, the same is also true. When we hide the shortcomings of our ancestors from our children, we may be making it impossible for them to compensate for or overcome a hereditary moral or spiritual problem. By omission, we condemn our children to repeat the generational cycles of restriction and loss.

4) **You may also have insights about your mate's family.** Tensions that affect you and your children may have originated from problems in your mate's family. Lifewriting can be the means for you to articulate these problems and to begin to resolve them just as you may have done for your own family. Airing the past, even if you choose to keep the writings private, is a healing activity.

5) **Lifewriting often promotes family unity by initiating many exchanges.** Consider the discussions you have with your children about your writing to be a primary means of transmitting your stories. Many workshop participants have reported that their commitment to writing has created occasions for them to sit with their children or their parents in a way they had not done in a long time.

Your children will ask you many questions and may even take exception to some of your insights. Just as they will reap rewards from your efforts, you, too, will benefit from their input. Because they are one generation removed from your parents and two from your grandparents, they may not be as emotionally involved as you are in the dynamics of those people's lives. Their emotional distance may provide a perspective you don't easily have access to on your own. Listening to others is an important lifewriting skill, too!

6) **Lifewriting often leads to personal growth** because writers feel empowered by the insights they derive from writing their stories. Some lifewriters have even said that the experience has liberated them. The insights you derive from writing will not leave you untouched.

Lifewriting can provide meaning and order as you deal with hidden fears and failings. However, like all long-term projects that are not quickly accomplished, there may be moments as you pursue personal growth through lifewriting when you will doubt both your ability to accomplish the task and whether it's worth doing. At such moments, I urge you to reread the mission statement you articulated in the previous section and to reaffirm your belief in the value of what you are doing.

> *"He who knows others is wise. He who knows himself is enlightened."*
> - Lao Tzu
> *philosopher*

Exercise

✔ Choose a positive characteristic that has run through your family for several generations (e.g., a commitment to hard work, generosity, manual dexterity).

✔ Make a list of all the individuals who have demonstrated this in their lives. How has it manifested itself in each of these individuals? An example with manual dexterity: "Uncle Frank was a mechanic, my sister Laura was handy at sewing, my son Bill is a carpenter.")

✔ Elaborate with details (e.g., "my son builds houses and furniture").

✔ Now write a short sketch of a moment when this trait was manifested in their lives. How has this characteristic been accepted or rejected by family members, by the wider community?

✔ Having done this for a positive characteristic, now choose a negative one and repeat the above exercise.

E. Scope: what's right for you?

In this section, you will be challenged to think about the breadth you would like your writing to have.

How much time and energy are you willing to give to lifewriting? The pleasure you will derive from your writing and the satisfaction you will feel in preserving your stories will depend on the honesty and perception you bring to answering this question.

The scope of your writing ambition is likely to change over the next months (often in favor of more rather than less time and energy). If you can formulate a realistic writing goal for yourself, doing so may well save you frustration and disappointment later.

1) **Do you have a definite idea of what you want to write about?**

- *my experiences in World War II*
- *raising my family*
- *the 10 most important events in my life*
- *the 20 most important events in my life and in my family*

If this type of statement reflects your thinking, then you have in mind a clear set of parameters you want to work within. It may be possible for you to write your stories in a few months with the help *Turning Memories Into Memoirs* can provide you.

When people get "hooked" on lifewriting, they often find that they expand on the scope of their original lifewriting ambitions.

2) **Are you a person who wants to write something more comprehensive**?

- *my life and its sociological, historical, cultural context*
- *my family's life and its historical context*
- *my community's history (sociological, economic, psychological)*

If this is the case, then you should be planning to continue working on your stories for many months or even a year or more. You will need a long time to write exten-sively and to do research on your material.

3) **Pacing is important**. If you overreach (try to write more than you have "wind" for), you may feel exhausted by the task. Instead of being a joy and a challenge, the work may feel too full of demands and responsibilities. You will grow to resent the project and may even feel you are a failure at it. This will make you very susceptible to giving up. You may say to yourself, "I guess I'm just not good enough at this!"

On the other hand, if you underreach (set too easy a goal for yourself), you may find the job not challenging enough to continue. If you do not go deep enough into why you did things in the past, if you avoid the difficult is-sues or events, if you record just facts and not feelings, you will find lifewriting unsatisfying. The demands of your life-- work, relationships, or obligations-- will rightly seem more important and you will abandon your writing pro-ject.

The best choice is to approach lifewriting as you might gardening: make your garden the right size for your en-ergy (your scope), locate it so as to give you regular, daily pleasure (collecting your work in an accessible notebook), fill it with the flowers you find most beautiful and the veg-etables you love to eat (your most important stories). Having done this, you will be rewarded with the many benefits of lifewriting and will eagerly persevere in your writing.

4) **Regularly assess your work in order to maximize your success.** From the start and continually throughout your writing project, keep asking yourself if the scope of your ambitions and the shape your work is taking is ap-propriate for you. Be willing to do what it takes to make the project a success for you.

Keep discarded sto-ries or story fragments in a manila folder. You may decide to rework the discarded pieces, or you may eventually revise parts of them to include in current writing. You may even now like them as is and can see where they fit! Consider everything you write as raw ma-terial which, with proper processing, will provide you with im-portant writing.

Exercise

✔ Write a statement of the scope you want your writing project to have. List the number of pages you hope to write; what years and people especially interest you; what historical, economic, and cultural features are to be included.

✔ Place this list near your mission statement in the front of your binder. Revise it regularly. Consider it as a contract with yourself to accomplish your lifewriting goals.

F. Make a schedule for success.

> This section is about structuring your writing time-- and about how absolutely necessary that is.

You've already taken several steps in lifewriting. You have begun to read this book and you have done some of the exercises. Now you need to take another step by establishing a writing schedule for yourself.

Rather than think in the general terms of "I'll write as much as I can" (who are we kidding!), base your writing schedule on a specific time or a page quota.

1) **Decide how much time per week you want (or have) to devote to lifewriting**. You may come up with a vague idea like: "Oh, five hours." If you don't push yourself to be more specific, you are likely to fail at writing your stories. If you want to succeed, *be specific*. Break your hours down to precise times on certain days.

Here's an example: "I feel I have five hours per week free in my schedule to devote to lifewriting. I will schedule two hours on Tuesday and Thursday from 8 AM to 10 AM and one hour on Friday from 4 PM to 5 PM."

> Guilt you feel doing something "just for yourself" can masquerade as a sense that there are more important things to do than write.

With that sort of schedule, you will not have to confess: "Time got away from me, and I didn't write at all this week!"

Eventually, as your schedule becomes a habit, you will have a sense of how many pages you can write in the time you have allotted. The pages will accumulate, and you will feel encouraged to continue writing. It will get easier and easier to write.

Sometimes people find it useful to set a date for finishing their work: Christmas, a family reunion, a wedding. Many writers report that a deadline (but keep it flexible!) helps them to stick to their schedules. It works even better if people expect your lifestories by your deadline!

2) **Determine how many pages per week you need to produce to feel you're making some progress**. This alternate way to get going is a variant of the above. Let's say you want to turn out five pages per week. Estimate how many hours it will take you to do that. Suppose you write roughly a page an hour. It will take five hours to meet your five-page quota. Now assign those five pages to five hours on specific days. Your schedule might look like this: three pages during the three hours on Monday from 8 AM to 11 AM and two pages during the two hours on Friday from 9 AM to 11 AM.

You can do that, can't you? But the rub here (which makes it a variant of the first suggestion) is that *you must continue to write past 11 AM on Monday or Friday if you have not met your page quota*! Conversely you may get up early from your writing desk to do something else once you produce your five pages (but I'm not encouraging you to do that-- why not write additional text that day?)

✐ **Whether you budget writing by the time or by the page, you do not have to write long, sophisticated stories.** Many lifewriters have produced short, journal-like entries for their loose-leaf binders every writing day. After a while, they collect and rework these entries into finished lifestories. This method keeps you producing while you develop the regular habit of writing.

3) **Either way-- approaching the task by the time or by the page-- be creative about your schedule.** A schedule is meant to maximize your chances for success. Both laxness and rigidity will work against you.

If you need to "borrow" time from your writing budget on any day, be sure you "pay it back" before you allow yourself to "borrow" again. Being lax with this "credit" system will set you up for discouragement and you could quickly feel overwhelmed (how easily and enjoyably can you "pay back" 30 hours?) or you'll find that you are kidding yourself-- you're no longer writing at all.

Being too rigid will also work against you. If your thoughts are flowing, you would do best to continue to write even if you have met your page or time quota for the day. Stopping in the middle of your creative process-- just because you have met your quota-- makes no sense whatsoever.

If you have a successful writing experience, duplicate the conditions-- for a while at least-- whenever you write. If a cup of coffee and classical music do the trick, make sure both are in good supply. If you need to work at a certain table, set yourself up there. If you write well at a certain time of day, clear your schedule. The unconscious is a powerful force, and it is frequently unleashed by the most trivial of stimuli.

"A lot of people talk about writing. The secret is to write, not talk."

- Jackie Collins
novelist

> Take writing step by step, day by day.
> **And remember: the work you are doing is important.**

Exercise

✔ Write up a detailed writing schedule for yourself. Be specific about dates, days, and hours.

✔ Enter this schedule in your calendar, and advise other members of your household about it. (Be willing to negotiate or to offer something they might want in exchange for their cooperation and support.)

✔ Pin the schedule to your family bulletin board or refrigerator so that you and they will be reminded of it.

Lifestories from the Workshops:

Sophia's Masterpiece by Leonore Burke

The following two lifestories say a lot about the people who wrote them. Start your own writing by recording a simple account of your own.

I folded the large *écru* lace tablecloth and held it to me before putting it away. Our dinner guests had admired the intricate workmanship of the Wheel of Fortune design, but for me, its delicate beauty was not its real value. What I cherished were the memories of my mother, Sophia Lazuk, crocheting it, over 45 years ago, by the table in the kitchen at 164 Chestnut Street, Chelsea, Massachusetts.

The kitchen was mother's domain. Mornings the sunlight streamed through the window over the sink. One pink and two purple violets flourished on the window sill. They were her only plants, and she cared for them tenderly. A small oval picture of the Holy Family hung between the windows by the red-and-white porcelain-topped table. In back of the table, chairs often held stacks of books and needlework supplies. Mother didn't seem to mind the clutter. The plain oak rocker by the black stove was the "loving chair". When Mother sat in it, she'd often invite my brother Albert or me to come sit on her lap. Sometimes we'd talk. Other times we'd just sit and Mother would hum and hold either or both of us in her arms. As she rocked, Mother often smiled and her otherwise ordinary features became beautiful. She knew how to make all of us feel good.

Just before Easter each year, mother would spend hours in the kitchen stuffing casing with her special *keilbasa* mixture, fragrant with garlic and spices. She kneaded the dough for the *placek*, a sweet Polish bread, on the kitchen table. My brother and I helped, as the *placek* required three separate kneadings. Flour would be everywhere. When it baked in the oven, the sweet aroma made our mouths water. Mother showed us how to dye the hard-boiled eggs in the food-coloring-and-vinegar mix, dipping them carefully and rolling them over and over for an even coating of rich color. On Easter morning after Mass at St. Stanislaus Church across the street, friends and relatives would arrive to share the Easter feast.

Mother's days started at 5:30, when she'd be up to make Papa's breakfast and lunch, and ended at about midnight when she returned from the second shift at Western Electric in Watertown, where she used her nimble mind and hands to assemble the complicated relay systems. Everyday for years, mother walked the seven blocks to *Babcia's* (Grandmother's) house to give her the insulin shot she needed and to do errands that were necessary. All day, Mother cooked and baked and cared

Leonore Lazuk Burke, who grew up in Chelsea, Massachusetts, was a legal secretary before her marriage. Motherhood promoted her to educator, chauffeur, and strategic planner for her four children's various activities. She now lives in South Harpswell, Maine, and is an avid tennis player, as are her children.

for all of us. I never heard her complain of having too much to do or of being tired. She always had time for a hug or two. Mother could get angry with provocation, but after she had said what she had to say, she would move to more important matters.

Mother had strong nimble hands and she enjoyed using them for crocheting. She created many beautiful colorful lace-trimmed handkerchiefs and pillow cases, bureau scarves and small items, often getting much pleasure by giving them to friends, relatives and neighbors. One day she decided to make a large special creation for me to have and enjoy when I would be an adult and have my own home. She started the large *écru* lace tablecloth with the Wheel of Fortune design. I remember watching her spread the work on the kitchen table. The silver hook grasped the thread and looped and pulled and twisted as the design took shape. She worked on it almost daily. It took a long time to complete as she had so little leisure time. One day a neighbor came to visit while my mother was working on it. She thought it was exquisite and offered my mother $300 for it. That was quite a sum in those days.

Mother smiled and said quietly, "I would never do this for money. I do it for love, for love." She was working on her masterpiece.

An Introduction to Education   *by Leland Davis*

Leland Davis' varied work life has included being a B-17 pilot, a high school principal and coach, an insurance and a real estate agent, and for ten years, a member of the Maine State legislature. Today he is president of the board of trustees of Monmouth Academy and vice-president and director of Community Service Communications, Inc.

From September 1947 to June 1948, I worked as a beginning teacher and coach. It was a challenging opportunity to help young people. My position, or should I say positions, were at Berwick Academy in South Berwick, Maine. Although a private school, it served as the public school for the youth of the area.

As the newest teacher on the faculty, I was given courses which veteran teachers didn't really want as part of their daily routine. I taught five different courses and monitored a study hall. I was also the vice-principal and the coach of boys' football, basketball, and baseball. When I wasn't teaching or coaching at school, I was preparing lessons and correcting papers at home. Needless to say, my wife of 20 months and daughter of 3 months didn't get a great deal of my attention.

However, I enjoyed working with students in the classroom and on the athletic field. Some were eager, some could care less, and some just went along for the ride. I had no difficulty finding good qualities in each of them. One young man in my business math class had started as a freshman three times and quit. His problem wasn't academic ability but boredom with the routine. I worked hard to keep his interest in school and he stayed with us for the full year.

My basketball team was rather successful, and I attribute its successes to the fact that four of the first five were left handed and thus frequently confused their opponents. We were runners up in our York County tournament so the community was very supportive of our accomplishments. It was really a joy but truthfully I felt my contribution to the successes was minimal.

My wife, daughter, and I lived in a huge apartment near the school. The first floor of this former sea captain's home housed the Home Economics Department and the second floor consisted of street side and back side apartments. My family occupied the front apartment and three single female teachers occupied the rear. These three veteran teachers were a good resource when we had questions about the school and community. We also had pleasant social gatherings when time permitted.

For a salary of $2,300 a year, it was an enlightening experience for a beginning teacher and his family.

Chapter 2   Getting Started

A.   *The backbone of your writing: lifelists*
B.   *Priming the pump of memory*
C.   *Where do I start?*
D.   *Memory jogs*
E.   *Dealing with pain*

Lifestories from the Workshops:
Into the Valley *by Florence Hodgkins*

Florence Odiorne Hodgkins' daughter Shirley plays on the spot where her mother ate her snack of bread & butter 20 years earlier.

A. The backbone of your writing: lifelists

If life teaches you anything, it's that you don't have inexhaustible energy and time. It is perfectly possible to run out of both before you get all your stories written.

With this in mind, you need to identify your most important lifestories-- the ones about the *prime* relationships and events of your life-- and concentrate on writing these first. They will serve as the backbone of your lifewriting. The peripheral stories will be recorded later-- as time and energy permit.

1) **Make a comprehensive *extended list* of the relationships and events which have shaped your life.** These are the relationships and events which, had they not occurred, your life (or the life of the person you are writing about-- your mother's or father's, etc.) would have taken a different turn. This is an *initial* list and it may be fairly long (with as many as one hundred or two hundred items on it). It is not unusual for a writer to spend two or three weeks compiling it. You will even find yourself adding to this list from time to time in the months ahead.

What kinds of items will appear on this extended lifelist? Here are a few:

- an illness or a death in the family
- the arrival of a sibling
- the community (town, neighborhood), the ethnic group, or the religious group you grew up in
- a fire, flood, tornado, automobile accident
- a relationship with an older person, or a peer
- a failure or a success at school-- scholarships, a decision to go or not to go to the university, a conflict with a teacher, having to leave school for work
- boyfriends/girlfriends, deciding to marry or not

This chapter will help you to identify the most important stories of your life and then guide you in the initial stages of writing them.

"I spent a whole week making lists. Was that lifewriting?"
- Workshop writer

- marriage
- children
- career choices
- religious, spiritual experiences

"A story comes into my mind. First, I feel it-- a gestation period. It kind of moves around and I feel it. Then I start to hear it. After that, I sit down and visualize it, and then I hunt for the perfect word that will describe what I see, what I hear, and what I feel."
- Hubert Selby
novelist

2) **Analyze the list you have compiled.** Are there relationships or events that you might group together in one category or under one heading? Would doing that make it easier for the reader to understand or evaluate these lifelist items? For instance, instead of scattering, or listing separately, the names of the men (or women) you dated from your eighteenth to your twenty-fourth year, you might cluster these relationships under a heading like "Getting ready to meet my husband/wife or mate". In this category, you might list the more significant relationships you had. This would create a natural occasion for you to write about how your understanding of what you needed in a mate matured over those years as you dated each of these people until you were finally ready to marry.

✐ **Rework your list.** Are all the items that can be grouped together organized under their appropriate headings? Doing this will make it easier for you to organize your material early on in the writing process and to draw clearer conclusions about the role or meaning of this material in your life. Your reader, too, will find it easier to understand your life if you organize your lifelist in this way.

Take your time, mull over your lifelist. Add or delete, combine or expand until you are satisfied that you have a list which is not only representative of your life history but which is organized to give a "bird's eye view" of your life.

"The {griot} began to recite the ancestral history of the Kinte clan, as it had been passed along orally down across centuries."
- Alex Haley
novelist

Your list, of course, includes specific names and dates (e.g., "deciding not to marry Roger T. in 1944", "the birth of my son David in 1963").

✐ **Feel free to add to your list at anytime.** Keep it open to additions whenever they occur to you. Placed in your three-ring binder with your stories, your list is handy so that you can refer to it.

3) **Narrow your list to ten relationships or events to create a** *core lifelist.* Having compiled this extended list, now select the most crucial events, the ones without which you would absolutely have become a different person than

who you are. Limiting yourself to ten items forces you to evaluate and select *the most significant* material to start writing about.

Based on the sample extended list above (see #1), here are some crucial items a particular writer might have chosen to include on a core lifelist. Notice that each of the following items not only mentions a plot-line (the *what*) but also includes the *consequences* for the writer:

> - the 1947 death of Nana Black who had always loved me unconditionally. I now felt alone in my family.
> - the flood that destroyed my father's print shop and thus forced me to reconsider and reduce my career options.
> - deciding not to marry Roger T. in 1944 because he drank, and deciding instead to go off by myself to be a hairdresser in Toronto which gave me a whole new sense of myself.

The *crucial* items on your core lifelist are almost never splashy events: not the time when you met a movie star briefly and superficially (e.g. Jimmy Stewart kissed you goodbye on the cheek when you both happened to be at the same railroad station in 1948!) but something essential like deciding (or deciding not) to move away or marry or like winning a scholarship and going to the university instead of into the mill (or vice versa).

By identifying core influences in your life, you can focus on them quickly in your lifewriting. In this way, early in your writing process, you will develop a significant body of stories that depict the person you are and have been. You will not squander time and energy on writing about secondary events in your life's evolution (perhaps you and your friends were impressed at the time by that Jimmy Stewart kiss at the railroad station, but has it really influenced your development as a person?). If you have the interest and the time, you can write about secondary events in your life later on. Otherwise, you may find yourself having run out of "breath" on the inessential stories before you have committed your core stories to paper.

"I wasn't ever a very observant person. Things just happened around me and I didn't really notice. So, what do I write about?"
- Workshop writer

Your stories are there waiting to be told. Your task is to let them emerge from the depths of your memory.

Exercise

✔ Write down at least twenty highlights (forty would be better, and eighty preferable) for your extended lifelist.

✔ Now create categories or headings under which to cluster different items.

✔ Lastly, compile a core list of the ten most crucial events, relationships, and decisions on your extended lifelist.

B. Priming the pump of memory

The next sections can go in an interchangeable order. This section will be helpful as you structure the content of your writing. Section C will help you write stories you have told before. Section D will help you to generate "new" memories.

People who attend *Turning Memories Into Memoirs* workshops will sometimes say, "I want to write my stories but I have forgotten so many details. Is there any way I can get them back?"

One answer that seems to work well is quite simple: by writing about your past, you will remember more and more of it! Like water pouring from a hand pump that has been primed, memories will begin to flow once you prime them with writing. As you write, from somewhere in your mind you may have thought you had no access to, memories will come to you. The more you write, the more you will remember. How it was to have a new sibling share your parents' attention... how your grandparents looked at each other across a room, their eyes full of love for one another... how insecurity tormented you at your first school dance-- this, and much more, will come back to you again once you prime the pump of memory.

1) **Write a lot, write frequently, and don't worry about whether or not your writing is "good enough"!** As you write, be comfortable with letting first drafts be first drafts: rough, incomplete, contradictory. Thinking in terms of "good enough" is a trap that will prevent you from writing

a lot and frequently. It will stop your ability to remember.

Unfortunately, we all have an *inner censor* judging our actions. It is the inner censor who asks if our writing is "good enough". It is our own censor who instills fear in us that we will look silly, who makes us hold back.

No one except the inner censor expects you to write deathless prose on your first attempts-- so tell your inner censor to relax! You are not competing for the Nobel Prize in Literature: you are "priming the pump" of your life-story writing.

If you haven't already written some pages of memories, select an item on your lifelist-- preferably your core lifelist. Pick up a pen. Now. Don't continue reading this book until you've written at least one page of remembrances.

In anything you do often and seriously, practice will make you better. That is just as true for writing as for any pursuit. Writing is a different skill from that of remembering, but developing skill at one will promote the other. The more you write, the more easily your memories will return to you.

2) **Write *vignettes*, *scenes*, *dialogue* without stopping now to figure out how they may eventually fit together**. Fitting your writing together will come in the rewriting stage. That is another, later step. But, at first, it's important to get text-- any text-- down on paper. Try writing on the backs of scrap paper cut into half sheets-- this is a trick to help free you from the false obligation of filling whole pages! Feeling obliged to fill whole finished pages can quickly make a drudgery out of writing.

Place your vignettes, scenes, and dialogue in an order that makes sense to you. Add more vignettes, scenes, or dialogue to fill in gaps in your story and make transitions ("...and because Uncle Boris came to America, I was able...") which show how all the separate components are connected to each other. What were disparate notes and jottings at first, with the help of fillers and transitions, will add up to readable, informative chapters of your lifestory.

If you are like many people I have worked with, you will find it easier to rewrite a text than to create the original material for that gaping, blank page. That's why *it's important to get your writing started*.

"Nothing you write, if you hope to be any good, will ever come out as you first hoped."
- Lillian Hellman
dramatist

"Writing is most of all an exercise in determination..."
- Tom Clancy
novelist

"...there are days when the result is so bad that no fewer than five revisions are required. In contrast, when I'm greatly inspired, only four revisions are needed."
- J.K. Galbraith
author

Your writing itself will be your most important writing teacher.

After you have many pages of text, the time will come for you to decide that this is better than that, to expand or make concise. This is editorial work, and it has its proper place in lifewriting-- but you are not yet at that stage of writing! Right now, you are priming the pump with first drafts. *Let first drafts be first drafts.*

3) **Remember: each stage of your writing will provide its own rewards and challenges.** Perfection is something to strive for later-- but not for now. At this early stage of lifewriting, retire the inner censor and strive for volume.

Exercise

If you find yourself anxious about writing, you may need to write about your early writing experiences. Did school, a particular teacher, or a relative make you too sensitive to the inner censor, too critical of yourself?

✔ Write about learning to write, about the history of your experience of writing. Might it have been penmanship or theme composition that closed you off? Did you face such constant criticism that it seemed impossible to have anything you wrote accepted by a critical teacher-- or was that the harsh voice of your own inner censor projecting itself? Become aware of your writing history by writing about it. To paraphrase a well-known statement: those who ignore their personal writing history are doomed to repeat it!

✔ If necessary, personify your inner censor. Imagine it as a little devil or a leprechaun. Clearly state to this figure that its presence is unwelcome and unnecessary. See (in your mind's eye) your inner censor turning away, disappearing, melting like the Wicked Witch of the West.

C. Where do I start?

1) **Most of us have a few family stories that we tell readily.** These are the stories we should write about first.

As you write, the process may seem spontaneous, the prose slips from your pen or appears on the computer screen! You may even wonder how you can write so easily, you who may not think of yourself as a writer and have put off writing all this while!

This is what has happened: over the years, you have rehearsed certain stories in your mind. They have been pared down to their essential components and reorganized for drama. Over time, when you told the story, it was obvious that you got better reactions from your listeners if you mentioned a certain item first and then built up to another item with specific transitions, etc. Is it any wonder that you are writing these stories now with relative ease? Most of the prep work on these stories was done ages ago!

These pieces are likely to be your best writing for a while. Enjoy the appreciation you receive from those with whom you share these "new" stories.

Pieces you write later may disappoint you by being much less polished than your first attempts. Remember that you will have spent only a few hours, rather than years, preparing to write these. Eventually, as you develop the craft of writing through repeated practice, you will write better stories at earlier moments in the process.

2) **Your first attempts at writing may also reveal memories you need to clarify or integrate into your life.** Often, the memories we have not resolved lie on the surface of our consciousness waiting for us to deal with them. When you sit down to start to write, these memories may "jump" at you and insist you write about them rather than about something else.

Here is an example of memories lying near the surface waiting to be dealt with. Do you know people who are tend to cry easily when they see something sad on TV? They do so not so much because they are more sensitive than others (that may be), but more likely because they harbor unresolved memories of their own past sorrows. Sad stories are excuses for them to mourn something in themselves they may not be fully aware of.

Lifewriting can be a healthy way to allow memories you have avoided to come to the surface. Committing them to paper may be a way to get free of their burdensome weight in your life.

"This poem came with practically no effort, and all of a piece. I was not surprised, though, for I had been obsessed with the subject matter for several months."
    - Joan Campbell
        poet

"Writing is easy: all you do is sit staring at a blank sheet of paper until drops of blood form on your forehead."
    - Gene Fowler
        writer

Exercise

✔ Write a family or personal memory that comes immediately to mind. As you write, don't attempt to censor your production or to channel it in certain directions.

✔ What might this tell you about yourself?

D. Memory Jogs

People sometimes wonder, "Am I starting to write at the right place?" The fact is: any place is the right place! Where you start is not as important as starting itself.

Here are a few "memory jogs"-- activities that will get you thinking and especially feeling about the people and places of your past.

1) **Scrutinize your photo albums.** Who are the people in your photos? What are their names? What are their relationships to you and to each other? What was happening to you and to them at the time of the photo? What do you remember about the place in which the photo was taken? Why were you there?

If you decide to preserve information on the back of photos, use a photosafe, soft lead marking or labeling pencil, such as an "All-Stabilo". Never write on the back of the photo using felt tip pens (they contain solvents) or ball points (they contain acid). Over time, these may bleed through to the front. Always write full names, full dates, and full locations. Never write just "Mary, Springfield, June", or "Jason, age 2". What is so obvious to you at the moment could be a mystery for generations to come!

2) **Take a mental photo.** Go back in time and "take" the photo you wish you had. Who is in it? How are they be posed? Describe the details: clothing, hair styles, setting. What happened right before this photo? right after? How did the people in the photo feel ?

3) **Look at photos and paintings of the time you want to remember and write about.** Study books and magazines on the history of fashions, of home decorations, etc. that deal with the relevant era. Also, visit vintage clothing shops, take in old movies, browse at flea markets.

4) **Make lists of members of your family**: their names, birthdays, principal residences, the type of schooling they had, their marriage dates, the number of children they had, their illnesses, jobs/careers, special events in their lives, circumstances surrounding their deaths, etc. You will find that focusing on uncovering this information for one member of your family will clarify facts about others-- or suggest areas you should explore. For instance, as you work out that Aunt Marie made that trip to New York in 19--, you'll realize that Uncle Eli couldn't have gone with her that summer because they didn't meet until two years later.

5) **Make lists from your past:** of both serious and frivolous items; of all your relatives; of record albums you have ever had or of hit songs you have liked; of movies, favorite dance steps, special foods; of anything else in your past that interests you. Then, write about the memories these lists evoke.

6) **Make opportunities to talk about the past with people who were there.** Stay clear of nostalgia and sentimentality. Look for facts, try to detect patterns and compulsions. Remember the good times. (See Chapter 4 on interviewing.)

"Sentimentality is the failure of emotion."
- Wallace Stevens
poet

7) **Write "time-capsule" descriptions of yourself and of anyone else you wish to include.** These descriptions should include physical, emotional, and spiritual considerations. Select various ages-- for example, at 20, at 40, at 60. When did noticeable differences in appearance and character occur? Are these differences attributable to age, to sickness, to an accident, to a reversal of fortune?

8) **Learn how to do** *visualization*. Visualization is a meditation-like experience in which a person calls forth ("visualizes") specific images (people, places, things). Through exercises, you can visualize, or call forth in your mind's eye, the images of your ancestors, of places where you have lived, of experiences that were important to you. Visualization can provide information your conscious mind may not even be aware of.

"Some of those memories are lost forever. How do you expect me to remember things that happened fifty years ago?"
- Workshop writer

Sometimes our sense of reserve keeps us from writing about others. Visualization can help us to ask "permission" from departed loved ones to inquire into, and write about, their lives. For many lifewriters, receiving "permission" frees them the discomfort they feel about probing into the lives of others.

However you need or choose to explain why visualization "works", it is a useful tool to open up your intuition and understand things about another person, about events you may have repressed in your memory.

Visualizations can be enormously creative experiences with many benefits. By all means find books on visualization and undertake the practices suggested (see Appendix B for reading suggestions).

"I don't remember anything. It happened so long ago that I've forgotten all the details."
- Workshop writer

9) **Write "letters" to someone-- now alive or dead-- you wish to write about.** Write as if you were composing a real letter. Ask specific questions. Share your thoughts and feelings. Now, answer your letter yourself as though your subject were writing back to you. Provide the answers to your questions, share his/her feelings and point of view. This correspondence may surprise you! It is your intuition that is tapping into your subconscious and giving you information and insight you didn't know you had.

These "letters" may also help you to recreate believable dialogue in your stories. The "letters" may contain favorite expressions and/or the diction (the style of speech) of the person you are writing about. Incorporating these into your stories will make your characters come alive.

10) **Journal writing can be invaluable to the lifewriter.** Its spontaneity and utterly private character help the writer to connect with her intuition and with her inner strength. The journal's honesty-- after all, who are you kidding but yourself if you alter the truth in your journal?-- can give you courage and practice to write honestly in your lifestories. The journal can also be an important source for lifewriting portraits and stories. Many people first explore issues and memories in the journal-- sometimes making several attempts at recording them before transcribing these into their lifestories.

E. Dealing with pain

Although delving into the past is a generally pleasant experience and promotes growth, it can sometimes be painful. This pain, if not handled well, can stop you from continuing with your writing.

Sometimes painful memories (poverty, childhood humiliation, abuse, abandonment, addiction, etc.) you had forgotten will surface. Or, you may be unwilling to evoke certain memories at all. Perhaps they are still too painful or perhaps you are afraid the pain will come back.

You might say, "I put that behind me years ago. I don't want to relive it." No one wishes you to resume gratuitously the pain which once had dominated your life.

This section will provide strategies for dealing with your painful memories.

But, if the memory is still so painful that you are afraid of reactivating it in your life, it's a message that you haven't gotten over the experience yet. It is still sapping your psychic energy-- whether you are consciously aware of it or not. Lifewriting may be very helpful to you.

✐ **The very act of writing about a painful experience can generate relief from the pain.** In a sense, your paper or notebook becomes a confidant, an ideal listener. Writing is an effective way of assuaging your pain and sometimes of freeing yourself of it once and for all.

✐ **Perhaps you can begin to approach your pain by writing around it.** For instance, if the death of your spouse is still too difficult for you to write about, you might try writing about when you first became aware of the signs of illness, about initial treatments when you were hopeful that a cure was possible.

"I put my story away. I can't write on it any more. Writing made me cry."
- Workshop writer

When you feel ready, give writing your difficult stories a try. Eventually, like peeling an onion layer by layer, you will come to the center of your grief-- and of acceptance and understanding. Though the process may be difficult, it will lead you to a new relationship with the memory, one cleansed of the pain that now surrounds it.

✐ **Writing your lifestories is not intended to be emotional or psychological therapy or a substitute for such work under the guidance of a professional psychologist.** Yet lifewriting sometimes conveys benefits very similar to therapy.

People would be well advised, in writing about painful memories, to think of a time when they were at the dentist. I know that I have sometimes had work done on my teeth without any painkiller being administered. I feel discomfort but no great pain. There have been other times, however, when I have started out without painkillers and then have grimaced with pain. When the dentist asks if I'm ok, I say an emphatic "No! I need help."

In writing about painful memories, there's a time when you know you can handle the experience alone. But when it's clear that you need some help, look for assistance from a professional whose expertise is to guide you safely through your pain.

Exercise

✔ Identify a past experience that is painful to you-- either because it was a loss, or an unresolved interaction, or because it caused you shame. Try writing a few sentences about the experience. Write only for as long as you feel comfortable.

✔ Now switch to writing a few sentences about what you will gain by exorcising this painful experience. Write about how it would feel to have your pain gone.

✔ When it feels right, continue writing about the painful experience until you feel you need to stop again. Allow yourself to return to this subject whenever it comes up for you until you have laid it to rest.

At the workshops

Roseanna had not spoken much except when I asked her a direct question, and then she answered with a simple yes *or* no. *In addition, she had not yet written anything to share with other members of the workshop.*

"I didn't go far in school," she'd say, "and I've never done much writing."

We were now at our half-way point in the workshops. At seventy-nine, Roseanna must have a lot of stories, but she was not sharing them. Would today be another no-writing session for her? Were we simply an afternoon's diversion for a lonely woman?

When I asked for volunteers to read their lifewriting assignments, Roseanna's hand shot up.

"Roseanna? You would like to read something?" I asked.

She reached into her voluminous purse and pulled out a handful of papers.

Slowly, she began to read her story. In it, she was a little girl of four. She lived in a small town and she told us about her life there, about her father who worked in the woods and made her little dolls when he was away in the lumber camps, and about her mother who had a beautiful voice and sang to the children at night. Then she told us about how suddenly she had to be very quiet because her father needed to rest. He was very sick. She was no longer allowed into his room much. Her grandmother moved in.

"Mama needed help with us because she was so busy nursing Papa," Roseanna said.

One day, he died. They put his body in the living room and a lot of people came.

His body was to be transported to the family cemetery plot some one hundred miles away.

"Mama and the baby accompanied his body. The rest of us stood with Nana at the station as the train pulled away with my daddy. I wanted him so much."

Tears streamed down Roseanna's cheeks. "Even after seventy-five years," she said, "it still hurts a lot."

We sat dazed, our eyes wet. We were in mourning for the little girl whose daddy had died.

Lifestories from the Workshops:

Into the Valley *by Florence Hodgkins*

Christmas 1918 was a good one for the Odiorne family of Greene, Maine. The World War was over and November, when Papa, Mama, Grammie, and I (Florence) had been oh-so-sick with influenza, was behind us. Best of all Mamma was home! The previous Christmas she had spent at Aunt Lillian's getting better from a bad operation. Grammie had been away too.

> In this lifestory, **Florence Odiorne Hodgkins** tells the painful story of her mother's death.

This year, when I was nine, things were as they should be. We were all at home, happy together. I was even daydreaming about next August when I would be 10 and no longer little. It would be the proper time, I decided, to begin to call Mama "Mother" like a grownup.

School began after New Year's for a six-week winter term. I walked as usual down the State Road to the Greene Corner School. It stood at the end of the Meadow Hill Road, next to Uncle Ed Rackley's hayfield. I had transferred there from the Patten School, now the Greene Fire Station, when it was time for Cousin Sylvia to start first grade. Seven pupils were needed to re-open the school, and I made the logical seventh.

Mrs. Addie Allen was our teacher. She lived a little farther down the State Road, past the cemeteries on either side of the road, just past the Universalist Church in the settlement known as Greene Corner. Before the coming of the railroad in 1849, and the moving of the post office to Greene Depot, this had been the center of town. Before the building of the mills in Lewiston, Greene Corner had been the local "metropolis". Lewiston children often came here in those early days for Greene Corner's superior school.

Mrs. Allen was a frail elderly lady, a good, kind teacher. She used, I remember, to spread her heavy winter coat out on top of the wooden book box and lie down to rest when we went outside to play at recess time.

January was a good normal time for us. Because the school was so near, Sylvia used to walk home for her noon dinner and I, as her cousin, was invited to accompany her.

I do not remember the last day of school that term. It is possible that our February vacation began a few days earlier than planned. However that may be, Mrs. Allen's chronic illness proved to be very serious, indeed. She died a few days later.

My own mother, Mary, had never been very strong. Life was not easy for homemakers in those days, especially in the country in the wintertime. Our kitchen was on the north side of the house. There was a black iron sink. At the right-hand end was an iron hand-pump sitting on a small shelf. This shelf also held a galvanized pail which was kept full of water. It was also used to fill the "reservoir". This was a square, nickle-plated, covered tank which was our everyday source of hot water. It had a permanent place on the right-hand back covers of the black iron Atlantic cookstove.

On cold winter nights, the sink spout always froze and very likely the water to the pump would catch also. One way to cope with that problem was to lift the pump handle higher than usual the last thing at night. Then we would listen as the water in the pipe ran back down below frost level underground. This meant a tedious job of priming the pump come morning. One did this by pouring water very slowly into the open top of the pump and, at the same time, working the handle vigorously until, at last, after a considerable amount of sputtering and gurgling, ice cold water poured out of the spout.

Thawing out the sink spout, however, was an outdoor job, and even more difficult. Papa always intended to handle that one, but barn chores and the care of animals came first. It was sometimes late in the day before it got done.

Wash day was a story unto itself!

That year, when Mamma had not been well, our laundry was sent to Beal's Wet Wash in the city. Members of the Beal family passed our house every day on the way to work and would pick it up and return it. We would then have the job of drying the wet clothes. Some families sent their laundry in town on the train packed in a galvanized tub.

On the second Sunday in February, my cousin, Hazel Wilkins, came home with me from Sunday School. After dinner, we were playing quietly because Mamma had a headache and was resting on the couch. After a time, she called me to her and said, "Florence, you and Hazel put on your things and go out and play. I think there's enough snow for sliding. Before you go across the road, run out in the barn and tell Papa I need him. You can fix yourselves a little lunch first if you want to." We hustled into our outdoor winter clothes, sliced some of Mamma's fresh yeast bread, spread it with home-churned butter and a generous coating of brown sugar. Then we hurried to the barn to deliver Mama's message.

On the south side of the road, opposite the old apple evaporator house, the level hayfield dropped off sharply, making a good little sliding spot-- safe but exciting. There we finished our snack and, I suppose, tried to play. It was a comfort to know that Papa would be in the house with Mama. He was the very best person to have near when you were sick.

Florence Odiorne Hodgkins was a teacher of mentally handicapped children for twenty-two years. She was born in 1909, in Greene, Maine, and still lives in her hometown.

Her headache was the beginning of what Dr. Hanscom called "brain fever", a complication of a second strain of influenza. She was the only one in the family affected this time.

By the next day, a trained nurse had come from one of the hospitals to take care of her. Each day she became a little weaker than the previous day. Mama died the very following Sunday.

I remember writing a letter to Grammie Odiorne and Aunt Lillian in which I mis-spelled the word *weak* using two *e*s. I felt so ashamed of this error. It seemed almost a desecration, a dishonor, to the one dearest to me in all the world.

I never did get to call her "Mother".

Chapter 3 Moving Your Stories Along

A. You can craft more effective stories.

B. How do stories come together?

C. Editing your work

Lifestories from the Workshops:
My Teacher: Dot Mehring by Dortha Faulls

Dortha Dust Faulls & family, 1921, newly arrived in New York City from Joplin, Missouri.

A. You can craft more effective stories.

It is not enough to *remember* your stories well. You need to *tell* them well also. In the same way that carpenters and cooks use techniques to heighten their chances of success, writers, too, have many techniques at their disposal.

Perhaps, like most lifewriters, you are passing your writing on to an innately-appreciative audience of relatives and friends. Naturally, your people want to encourage your efforts and tell you how wonderful your writing is. This doesn't relieve you of the obligation to write well! Craft your stories as carefully as possible. Don't make it difficult for people to shower you with accolades!

Learning to handle the writing techniques that follow will help you to craft more effective stories.

1) **The people you choose to write about in your stories are your** *characters* (either you or someone else). Although they may be familiar to you, people you've loved and known, your characters are often strangers to your children and grandchildren-- your likely targeted audience.

You can make your reader "see" your characters by writing about them with *specific and striking details:* what did they look like (hair color, height, the style of their walk)? what did they wear (colors, textures, styles-- how did they wear their clothing, what was their bearing)? You can help your reader to "hear" these people whose voices perhaps still resonate in your ears: make extensive use of dialogue that was authentic to your people-- favorite words and sayings, even phonetic transcriptions (writing according to sound rather than grammar). Create windows on your characters' inner lives by giving us glimpses of how they felt. (If you practice visualization as mentioned in the previous chapter, you may find it very useful

This chapter will help you write better stories than you had ever thought possible.

"No ideas but in things..."
        - W.C. Williams
                poet

here.)

✒ **The people and the culture of your childhood are as foreign to your children and/or grandchildren as are the people and the culture of Outer Mongolia!** Don't ever take it for granted that anyone is familiar with what you are writing about. Instead, assume no one knows anything. Portray your characters and their lives patiently and minutely with specific and striking details.

Here is a graphic example of the misunderstanding the lack of detail can lead to. You write a piece meant for your grandchildren to appreciate how hardworking your mother was on Monday washdays: she would heat water for the wash, set out a variety of tubs for the different assortments of laundry, use a hand wringer propelled by muscle power, and hang everything out on a line-- even in winter. You remember so clearly how the all-day job left her exhausted by evening. You feel that this is important information for your grandchildren to know about their great-grandmother, and so this is what you write as part of one of your lifestories: "My mother did the entire wash on Mondays when I was a child. Boy, was it a lot of work!"

Reading the story of your mother, your grandchildren conclude that Great-grandma dropped the colored wash in the automatic washing machine, pressed a button, and then sat down to listen to a soap opera on radio (perhaps they know there was no TV then!). Forty-five minutes later, when the buzzer went off, she transferred the wash to the dryer, put a load of whites into the machine, and then retired to listen to more soap operas! "What's the big deal?" they might want to ask you-- but won't because they don't want to hurt your feelings!

The "big deal" is that you have presumed too much from your readers. You have to suppose, instead, that your readers know nothing about your characters or the world they lived in! So, if you want them to appreciate your mother's hard work, go back to your Monday wash scene and describe heating water on the stove, and setting the various tubs out on various kitchen surfaces, etc. Don't *tell* us washday was a lot of work-- *show* us by using specific and striking details. Lots of them.

2) **What your characters do or what happens to them is the *action* of your story.** The action need not be dra-

> *"Pay attention. To everything... how (your characters) walk, talk, sing, eat, dress, dance, sleep, frown, twitch, yell, fight, cry."*
> *- Marta Randall*
> *novelist*

> *Each new generation is a horde of barbarians that has to be assimilated into the existing adult culture.*

matic (life's quiet moments make good stories too) but it should be written so as to make your readers want to know what happens next (this is often achieved through *suspense*-- hinting at something to come). You will make them turn pages, from one story to the other.

Another word for action is *plot*. An action or plot most frequently needs a *beginning* in which the conflict is set up, a *middle* in which the conflict gets more complicated, and an *ending* in which the conflict is resolved or at least brought to a close.

✐ **Start your action close to the final** *crisis point* **or** *climax*. This is the point (which you now know from hindsight) where things came together or fell apart for the people (the characters) in your story. Starting close to the crisis point (climax) and proceeding inevitably towards the ending will enable you to sustain the suspense needed to keep your reader "hooked". (One technique to achieve this is to use an early sentence like "I didn't know it then but that day was to change my life...")

Here is an example of starting close to the crisis point. If you are writing about your divorce, don't start with the first kiss you shared in high school. (That might make an interesting story, but for another piece with its own crisis point: perhaps your realization that you were in love?) Instead, a divorce story could start with your awareness that you needed marital counseling after eighteen years of marriage. You'd proceed with the collapse of the sessions and your painful acknowledgment that this is a marriage that will have to end (these are crisis points-- the final crisis point or climax comes when you and your mate confront each other). The *turning point* comes with the divorce going through and your facing an uncertain future.

✐ *Show action, don't tell it. This can hardly be overemphasized!* The reader needs to "see" your characters in actions that will reinforce what you are saying about their personalities and temperaments. Don't only tell how nurturing your father was. Show him *doing* something nurturing in your story. You have to show us the action that backs up a statement. Better yet, skip your statement and just *show* us the action! **We can draw our own conclusion about your father.** *When you tell rather than show, you take away from the drama of your story.*

It is action which gives drama to information.

"Tell a story! Don't try to impress your reader with style or vocabulary or neatly turned phrases. Tell the story first!"
- Anne McCaffrey
novelist

✐ **Convey the important information of your lifestory in action form**.

A) The following example contains all the facts you want to relate to your reader.

On our farm in 1939 we had three Guernseys, one Jersey, four Holsteins, six pigs, 32 chickens. Our house had two stories. We slept upstairs, and the rooms were not heated. My mother had an Atlantic stove. She made pancakes in the morning. I liked pancakes and oatmeal and waffles. The school was two miles away. We walked there with our family and friends. Our teacher was Miss Lindstrom. When I attended that school, I won a scholarship to attend the local academy.

B) This next example also contains all the facts, but it does something else: it transmits the facts in action form.

We would wake up in the morning when my mother would shout up from downstairs, "Five-thirty!" The bedrooms were not heated so as soon as we opened our eyes we could see our breath congealed in the frozen air. We snuggled into our blankets, postponing getting up in the cold room for as long as we could.

"Tell a good story. And let it bring your characters to a different place (in soul and/or body) than where they started out."
- Catherine Breslin
writer

"Get up quick, boys" Mother would say. "Miss Lindstrom won't tolerate your being late, and Father needs help with the milking before you eat breakfast."

We would run downstairs and dress next to the warm Atlantic stove. We had left our clothing there at night to be warm in the morning.

"When you get back, I'll have pancakes ready for you," Mother said. Pancakes were my favorite breakfast, followed by oatmeal and waffles.

We rushed out across the yard to the barn.

"Do you think you'll find out today?" asked Jim.

I had applied for a scholarship to our local academy and Miss Lindstrom had said she thought she would have an answer for me that day at school. As my brother and I started with the milking, I fantasized what it might be like to study at the local academy.

There were three Guernseys, one Jersey, and four Holsteins to milk so the chores took us a while to finish. My father was feeding the pigs. There were six as well as the 32 chickens...

The second example provides all the information you want to impart but it does so in a more dramatic manner than the first example. The second example transmits its facts in the guise of the action of a *typical (rather than actual)* morning. It also has an element of *suspense*. The reader will be kept wondering about the scholarship until he gets to the point at which Miss Lindstrom reveals the good news. The moment before she spoke, when you knew she was about to but did not know what she would say, would be the *final crisis point* or *climax*. In this second story example, you convey a lot of information and create a successful story by making use of **character, action (beginning, middle, and end), setting** (see subsection #3 below for information on setting), and **suspense.**

 ✐ **Choose a few of the clearest, most eloquent details to convey your ideas--** *and always do it with action.* Demonstrate your point with three to five examples *at most*-- better yet, put forth two or three. More examples would be overkill-- and potentially boring. If you simply must include more examples, go ahead and indulge yourself. After you've gotten them off your chest, however, eliminate all but the *few* best examples from your text, keeping only the most eloquent ones.

 You must decide to write about the most important aspects of your life and to leave out a lot of peripheral material if you want to engage and retain your reader's interest. Effective lifewriting records the gist (the essence) of your lifestories. Sooner or later, lifewriters must accept that they cannot tell everything that happened to them-- it would simply be too long a story both to write and to read.

 3) **The *setting* is the environment in which your characters live and in which your action occurs.** The setting includes the *place* (geography, buildings, interiors), the *time* (year, month, day, hour), and the *atmosphere* (mood, feeling, ethnic culture, religion, educational levels, etc.) Setting is crucial for interpreting character. It is often the most inaccessible element for your younger readers, the element which they need however to interpret your story.

 ✐ **Be specific in describing your setting:** avoid abstract words and phrases! Because abstract words and phrases are vague, they conjure quite different images for different people. Specific and striking details, on the other hand, are more likely to mean nearly the same things to different people and so help your story to mean what you want it to mean.

Writing is like swimming. To do either right, you have to do everything together. But you can only practice one thing at a time. One day, you start doing several techniques at once and then it all comes together for you!

Don't use vague, abstract phrases like *majestic mountain*. Be more precise in your observation. If the mountain is capped with granite and has two peaks, you might write: *twin, granite-capped peaks*. If the mountain is completely forested over with pines, you might write: *covered with pointed pines*.

Although the reader will always bring his own interpretation and experience to your writing, your details will guide his perceptions in a way that abstract words cannot.

✏ **Make ample references to the senses.** We need to know what something *tasted* like, what it *smelled* like, *looked* like, *sounded* like, *felt* like. Again, avoid using abstract words (e.g., a *fragrant* odor) in favor of very tangible, sensual ones (the odor of *wet pine needles*). *Sense references* lend your readers the illusion that the story is being lived as they are reading it, that it is their first-hand experience.

4) **Keep your individual stories focused on only one set of characters, actions, and settings.** Asides, or digressions, however scintillating they may be, change the focus and therefore subtract from the impact of a story. They tend to confuse because they include extraneous and complicating details or they tend to bore because they go on and on. Digressions are often "stories within a story". If they really are good stories, give them their own billing. Otherwise, cut them out.

5) **Your stories will have a *point of view*** in addition to character, action, and setting. Point of view is a technical term in writing. It refers to the "eyes" of the narrator from which the story is seen or perceived.

For example, if you are telling a story of when you were five from the point of view of the child you were then, your text will be written in "five-year-old" talk as if the five-year-old had written it or were speaking it. Obviously, the piece will contain different insights and vocabulary than the same story told from the point of view of the adult you are now.

✏ **The point of view you select will help you to achieve certain effects**. The story of your childhood written from a child's point of view will have more intimacy but will necessarily lack the adult's understanding of life. If you tell the same story from your adult point of view, however, although you will lose intimacy, you will be able

Style (in the sense of uniqueness) is something most writers think about too much. It is more appropriate to worry about such elements as clarity *and* coherence *than about* style.

to create a "bigger" picture that contains the consequences of what happened and your adult interpretation of your parents or other adults. For instance, an adult can write about the sources of (reasons for) a family's financial woes; a child can only write about the *effects* of those financial problems.

Every story is told from a point of view: as a writer, you must be aware of that. If you don't consciously choose one, you will most likely write out of the point of view of the adult you are now-- this may or may not be appropriate. If you lose track of your point of view-- either forget to choose one or alter it within the story, you may write some things that don't make sense: like making an adult interpretation or using an adult vocabulary in what is a story told from a child's point of view. Be aware of choosing and making consistent use of a point of view before you start writing.

*The point of view will also help set the *tone* of your stories*. The tone is the story's emotional slant. It influences how the reader will feel about your story. Possible tones include: pity, admiration, empathy. Besides being affected by the point of view, the tone is dependent on *vocabulary, images, metaphors*, and *organization of the text*. Often, when the reader does not feel what the writer hoped he would, the problem is one of tone. For instance, it's more difficult for me to feel empathy with "a hard-hitting gal" but much easier to feel rapport with "a woman who faced life's challenges with hope and courage." The tone itself has changed my feeling for the character.

Your point of view (and consequently the tone) will also largely determine how the reader will interpret your stories. Point of view is a powerful writing tool. Your sympathy or antipathy for your subject will dictate choice of detail, of description, of action. It will ennoble or degrade your subject. Sometimes, the same characteristics and qualities can be presented as nearly opposites in their meaning-- depending on the writer's choice. For instance, a writer can say of a person who speaks a lot "she foamed at the mouth" or "she was doing her thinking out loud". If the writer believes in the virtues of hard work, she can write, "Hard work helped my mother arrive at frugality"; but, if she doesn't, she can write "Hard work bludgeoned

"I wanted to recapture the fear I felt then as a little boy. I wanted my readers to experience how I felt so I wrote from a ten-year-old's point of view."

- Workshop writer

The re-writing stage can be the most creative part of writing. Re-writing is often the time when you begin to understand what it is you are really writing about. In re-writing, you may also realize what it is you actually want or need to say.

my mother until she became a skinflint". An action that requires out-of-the-ordinary energy can be labelled "courageous" or "foolhardy".

Although we inevitably write from our own points of view and so are always interpreting from our own perspectives, it is possible to write without *imposing* an interpretation on others. For example, you can write: *My mother was young and she found it difficult to fulfill her maternal responsibilities. I remember being a little child and wanting her to be more attentive to me* instead of writing *Always forsaking her basic duties for her own selfish pleasures, my mother abandoned us emotionally as only the most heartless of hussies could. Everyone in my family felt lonely and resentful.*

The first example shows how *you* felt. One does not get the impression you are "throwing stones". How can anyone argue with that point of view? It's yours and you're entitled to it even if someone else disagrees.

The second example, however, is very judgmental and makes a sweeping statement that smacks of your need for revenge. Can readers be blamed for feeling that they are being corralled onto your side?

Abusing point of view like this will alienate your reader and be counterproductive to your goal: sharing your lifestories and experiences with your audience.

Realize that you can exercise choice about point of view anytime you want to achieve the effects you are striving for, but remember that manipulating your readers can also backfire on you and cause them to resent being corralled onto your side of an issue.

In addition, remember that consistency in point of view will strengthen the impact of your story while slipping back and forth from one point of view to another will distract the reader and weaken your story.

Exercise

Evaluate the stories you have already written from the perspective of character, action, setting, and point of view.

✔ Are your characters described in detail? Do you mention what they looked like, what they wore and said, *how* they said it?

✔ Have you started your stories *close enough to their climaxes*? Did you *show* the actions of your stories rather than *tell* them?

✔ Have you focused your story on *one set* of characters, actions, and settings? Have you avoided abstract words in favor of specific, descriptive ones?

✔ Are you conscious of what *point of view* you have used? Is it the most effective point of view you could have chosen? Is it consistent throughout?

✔ Have you chosen the right *tone* for each of your stories? Look at how your language may be value-laden. Do you abuse the power of the technique of point of view by trying to get the reader on your side?

Make changes to improve your stories wherever you can. **Remember: the time you spend rewriting is an opportunity for you to do your best work.**

B. How do stories come together?

1) As you write, think in terms of *vignettes* or brief stories that run to only a few pages. Don't worry about how to link these pieces. Instead, write as if you were creating separate movie takes. Each "take" is a discrete piece of the story with its own *character, action*, and *setting*. In the making of a movie, these "takes" eventually get spliced together into a full-length product-- the work of a film editor who organizes the separate scenes to make a whole. Your vignettes and brief stories, too, will be "spliced" together (by you!) into a satisfying and unified story-- but that will come later.

✐ **It is easier, and therefore perhaps more useful to achieving your writing goals, to try to write *many* stories rather than to try to write *long* stories.** Don't let yourself be paralyzed by the fear of having to write long stories.

Keep your work in the process stage for as long as you can. If you consider your writing to be a finished product too soon, you'll feel it can't, or shouldn't, be reworked when, in fact, it may need it.

Now frankly, *anyone* would be daunted by the prospect of a project that entailed describing entire periods of one's life-- and even one's whole life, but *everyone* can write a few pages about a first job or the birth of a child.

(As I undertook the writing of this book, for instance, I started by jotting notes on various topics. Eventually, I grouped notes on similar topics together. This section, written on the backs of scrap paper, was labelled "Writing organization". At first, it consisted of only two half-pages.)

Your two and three page stories, if there are 20 or 30 of them, do add up to 40 and 60 pages of text and, if there are a hundred of them, to 200 and 300 pages of text.

2) You will have options in organizing your material. Eventually, of course, after you have written a while and have amassed a pile of stories, you will want to group them together so as to make a statement, a total picture. How will you do it? Below are ideas for organizing your stories.

Note: These suggestions do not refer to the order in which the stories are written but only to how they can be organized after they have been written.

✐ Chronological

If you choose a chronological order, you organize your stories in a way that most nearly replicates the sequence in which events happened. For example, what happened in your childhood is placed first in the narration and what happened in your youth is placed second and your middle-age third; what happened in the spring is placed first, in the summer second, etc. If you organize all your stories in this way, there will be a natural continuum among them based on time connection. *This is the way most people choose to link their stories.*

✐ Thematic

You might choose to put together specific topics across the generations or among family members. These topics might include religion, careers, marriage, etc. For example, you might look at the relationship to work in your family during your childhood. You might write about your grandparents' and your parents' work attitudes and practices during this time. Then you can give your attention to other themes in their lives during your childhood: parenting, religion, etc.

Another possibility is to write about a theme in your grandparents' lives and then go on to its appearance in your parents' lives and then in yours and lastly in your children's. You can choose to give an internal chronological development to each of your themes: start with youth and proceed to old age or the present with each generation. Then start the whole process over again with another theme.

✐ **Biographical**

Take one person through his/her life and then take another person through. This allows for both chronological and thematic development.

✐ **All of the above**

Although you may begin to write your pieces chronologically, thematically, or biographically, you may find yourself combining all of these elements in your final product. These approaches can easily be integrated into your lifestory as a whole.

Exercise

Take a look at the stories you have already written.

✔ Place them in your looseleaf notebook in an order that makes most sense to you now and become aware of the order your stories are taking.

✔ Assess where there may be large gaps in the links between your stories or where you just need to add a transition story or two.

✔ Make a list of missing story links that you would like to include. This list will provide you with material to write about when you sit down to a blank page. You certainly won't have to worry about "writer's block" with this list in hand!

C. Editing your work

The secret to editing is to read your manuscript as your reader will-- with fresh, observant eyes. This is another

In this section, you will learn a few techniques that will help you to act as your own editor.

"I put (the poem) away for a week or two until I have forgotten about it and can take it up as if it was something entirely fresh.
- Wallace Stevens
poet

"I understand my own pictures best six months after I have done them."
- Pablo Picasso
painter

way of saying you need to develop a certain objectivity to edit your work effectively. How can you do this?

1) **Put your writing aside for a while**. After you have written a story or a scene or a chapter of your lifestory, put it away. Time-- two weeks, a month, six months-- will give you the emotional distance to assess your work more objectively and will help you to identify both its strengths and its shortcomings where more work is needed. If your piece seems strong to you under this test, congratulate yourself! And keep writing.

I regularly put my work away for a while (for a week, a month, or even a year). I am always amazed at how much objectivity I can manage to muster when I reread my work after a lapse of time. For a moment, I really do step into the role of the reader and out of that of the writer of the piece.

✐ Sometimes, to make re-reading easier, it can even be useful to play a certain role. Approach your manuscript from the point of view of some person who might be censorious of your writing (but not your inner censor who is more likely to criticize you than the work itself). Ad-lib something like: "Let's see what have we here? Humph! A story by So-and-So. I wonder if it's any good?" Then read the piece from this critical perspective. Does it stand up to this scrutiny? If the text doesn't, consider yourself lucky to have the opportunity to make the necessary changes to improve it.

2) **Show your manuscript to others** for their criticism. Family members can be a good choice because they may be able to add important information and details to your story.

Be careful, however, to choose people who will critique the work itself rather than you. You also need to protect yourself from someone who says, "Why are you doing this hard work? Why don't you just enjoy yourself at your age!" Conversely, the blindly-supportive "Isn't that nice, dear, I like anything you do!" response isn't at all constructive either!

Be on the look-out, too, for someone who might want to slant the story toward *their* interpretation of an event or relationship in order to substantiate their point of view rather than yours. (Let them write their own lifestory if they have something different to say!)

All feedback can, however, teach you something. A disagreement with a relative about slanting a story might tell you that you have not conveyed what happened with enough objectivity. Sometimes, you can do this by providing several sides to a story. You can write something like, "According to my brother John, our mother was a strict disciplinarian... but according to me, she..."

Others who are not relatives-- friends, colleagues-- may also be able to provide you with valuable feedback that is different from your relatives'. It may come in many forms. "I don't really understand why your mother did this. It really seems out of character for the portrait you have drawn of her." Your reader might ask, "Why did your father say that? It's not clear to me why you interpret it as supportive of you. He comes across as very cold to me."

Perhaps your technique was faulty and you will need to rewrite. Perhaps your portrait was a family-sanctioned view which you unconsciously superimposed on your own experience of events! Writing that is based on unexamined versions of events or relationships is almost always confusing to others (who are not relatives with the same "blind" slant as yours). With a sudden flash of understanding, you will recognize the truth pointed out by these questions and comments that seems so obvious to someone more objective.

✐ **If you have to explain, you probably need to spend more time re-writing your text.**

Remember: you will not be with the reader to answer questions every time the piece is read. Your story needs to be so clear that it answers its own questions. Your childhood or youth culture (what life was like when you were young in your family and in your community) is perhaps foreign to everyone but yourself!

3) **If you don't have time to put your stories away or to send them to someone who can do a critique, at least read them out loud-- to yourself first and then perhaps to someone else.** Hearing your words will make you more objective about your text. Again, it will be as if you were an observer, a stranger.

A variant of reading out loud is to read your stories onto a tape and then play the recording back to yourself.

Don't be discouraged if you see the need for changes in your stories. Most successful writers are persevering re-writers who see re-writing as an opportunity to accomplish the real work of writing.

"Speak your dialogue out loud. If it sounds like the way people talk, then write it down."
- Tom Clancy
novelist

"Respect your reader. The niftiest turn of phrase, the most elegant flight of rhetorical fancy, isn't worth beans next to a clear thought clearly expressed."
- Jeff Greenfield
columnist

Simplicity is often the key to clear communications.

Hearing your story will enable you to play the listener for a while. Doing this, you can learn a lot about how effectively your writing communicates.

Reading aloud you will notice whether you are trying to use big words or flowery words. Sometimes people who are not experienced in writing feel that, to achieve quality in their work, they need to use "literary" words. Out of the pens of these writers come words and phrases now found only in English romance novels or words barely remembered from some high school poetry class. Resist the urge to use such big or literary words.

Sometimes, as you read aloud, you will notice yourself tripping over some of your sentences. Is this because you are using long or convoluted sentences? As a rule, shorter sentences are better than longer ones. Shorter sentences are easier to write and to read. As readers, we don't like long, rambling sentences that require several readings to get through.

✐ **Here's a rule of thumb: after about 15 words, think of adding a period! You'd better have a good reason not to start thinking of ending that sentence!**

Exercise

How do you edit your writing?

✔ Do you keep the editing function for one of the last things you do when you write or do you edit as you go along? Which way feels better? Which way keeps the inner censor quiet longer?

✔ Try each of the editing techniques outlined in this section. How does each feel? Which are you going to continue using?

Lifestories from the Workshops:

My Teacher: Dot Mehring by Dortha Faulls

This is a deeply felt story about a mentor and her role in the author's life. It was substantially rewritten after members of the author's TMIM workshop group gave her their feedback in class.

After Sunday School class, my teacher, Dot Mehring, stopped me at the head of the stairs and told the other girls to go on down. Miss Mehring was tall, statuesque, and wore thick glasses. Her low-pitched voice seemed to constantly say something important. I always listened to her every word.

"What's wrong?" she asked, as she leaned against the wall and pulled me to her side. She put both arms around me and leaned over to hear my answer. I was immobilized, frozen, hardly able to speak.

Finally, I said, "I'm late."

It was the time of year to change the hour on the clocks and nobody had done it at our home the night before. Until now, I had had a perfect attendance record and I didn't want to lose it. But I was late. Would this mean an absence on my record?

As soon as I had told her, "I'm late", I realized the tense was wrong. I should have said "was".

"It doesn't matter," she said. "Next Sunday, you'll be on time."

We walked down the stairs, her arm around me, and I was in heaven again. Because the mistake had not been mine, I was allowed to keep my perfect attendance record.

Dot Mehring never once said to me, "You should go to college", but she somehow imparted to me the resolve to do this, against many odds. This dynamic woman took the place of something that was missing in my life. No one in my family had ever gone beyond high school. But Miss Mehring had received a master's degree and a doctorate from Columbia University.

Born in Missouri, **Dortha Dust Faulls** *grew up in New York City. Like her mentor, she was a teacher for many years.*

She had inherited some money from her parents and so was able to provide our class with many unusual experiences we would not have had otherwise. Our parents could hardly afford to raise us, let alone do for us what she enjoyed doing. She took us to our first Broadway show in New York. She took us to visit International House where many foreign students lived. We went to a Chinese restaurant and ate with chopsticks. She took us on picnics and cookouts.

One day she took us to a corner drugstore for ice cream

sodas. Another girl's brother, Jimmy, who had recently started college, was with us. It made a big impression on me: to think that this boy, whose sister I knew, was actually going to college!

That summer, Dot Mehring toured Europe. She sent a postcard to each girl in her Sunday School class. I cherished mine for months, perhaps even years. At the time, I was so intent on saving my nickels and dimes for a trip of my own that I overlooked the significance of the card she had selected for me. It was a picture of "Big Ben", the huge clock tower in London.

She may have meant to show me the importance of knowing the correct time. But I really think she wanted to remind me of our shared moment, that Sunday when I had been so late.

My cache of nickels and dimes never gave me a trip to Europe. However, I did manage, through financial help from an uncle, to go to college.

I will never forget Dot Mehring.

Chapter 4 Interviewing and Research

A. Before the interview
B. At the interview
C. Doing academic research
D. Taking research notes
E. Assuring access to your information
F. Non-academic research

Lifestories from the Workshops:
Black Saturday by Joseph Croteau

Interviewing and research

People sometimes think they can trust their memories when they write their lifestories-- but memory isn't always as reliable as you want it to be! It can either fail you completely or mislead you. Of course, you may also simply never have had the information you need to write about an event or another person with any kind of depth. Sometimes too, you may lack the perspective that can only be had through feedback from another person or source.

Interviewing and research will supplement your memory. In addition, they will support the facts and impressions that memory recalls.

Interviews are basically guided conversations as you sit with people and talk with them. *Research* is acquiring information from non-human sources.

This chapter will help you to conduct family interviews and to get the most out of the research you collect.

A. Before the interview

1) **Carefully select whom you will interview**. If your time is limited, or your family is large, it will be all the more important for you to identify a small number of knowledgeable relatives and friends to interview.

✐ For example, Aunt Mary tends to talk endlessly-- all afternoon if you let her. Her conversation seems to have little content as she wanders from one topic to another. Aunt Jane, on the other hand, is an incisive person whose intuition is always informing her about what things mean. Her observations and reminiscences are always interestingly told.

Can there be any doubt whom you will interview first-- Aunt Mary or Aunt Jane? (Being nice to lonely Aunt Mary

is a work of charity and it should not be confused with collecting information to write your stories.)

✐ Another example: Cousin Luigi married into your Irish family. He is a dear old man and you love him very much, but his tales about his Italian family are irrelevant to understanding the history of your Irish ancestors. His are not the accounts you need to collect-- unless, of course, Cousin Luigi took you into his home after you were orphaned and, as a result of growing up in his house, you were culturally Italian-American and not Irish-American. Your emotional inheritance, in this case, would be derived from your adoptive Italian ancestors and not your biological Irish ones! In fact, if this particular hypothesis were true for you, Uncle Luigi's stories become *very* important to knowing who you are.

2) **Make clear and specific preliminary arrangements with the people you will interview.** Be specific about the meeting time, the length of the interview, the place where it will occur, and the conditions necessary for its success. It is often useful to have the interviewee gather *memory jogs* (photos, clippings, mementos-- see Chapter 2, Section D) to use as warm-ups to start the interview.

Be very specific in your requests. Broad requests like "We'll need a good amount of time" can be interpreted so differently that they are useless in making arrangements. Instead say, "We'll need a two-hour block on Tuesday the fifth from 2 PM to 4 PM." If you say, "Is there a room in your house where we can talk quietly?", it is possible that your interviewee will say *yes* in spite of the fact that she knows someone will be watching television or working in that room ("They'll just be listening to their program"). You need to say, "We have to have a space where no other activity will be going on-- no TV, no radio, no telephone conversations, no work." If your interviewee says there are no such rooms in her house, perhaps you can suggest meeting at your place. I have found that I cannot be too specific about the details. A crucial one left out of planning, or ineffectively decided, can sabotage your interview.

✐ If you have any reason to suspect that your communications were not clear to your interviewee, state your needs once again. *Nuances have no place when you're setting conditions.* Protect yourself from wasting time, time during which you could be writing.

3) **Ascertain who else is likely to want to participate in the interview-- and decide whether that person may or may not sit in.** An unexpected, or inappropriate, person can deflect the focus from the topics you have come to gather information about.

For instance, your aunt by marriage may sit in on the interview and find what you are doing so interesting that she begins to talk about *her* life experiences and in doing so may not allow your uncle (your mother's brother) much time to talk about his childhood relationship with your grandparents and your mother. Your aunt's experience, however interesting it may be, will not provide the information you need to understand your grandparents and parents.

✐ Conversely, don't dismiss other people's input too quickly. Their experiences can be true of your family, too. By listening carefully to an articulate person talk about a general experience, you might learn a lot about your own family. For example, you are interviewing your mother's brother when his wife (your aunt by marriage) begins talking about her family. It's likely you didn't know these people she's talking about, and their personal lives don't fit into your story. As your aunt shares her stories, however, you realize that many of them are about work in and life around the mining towns of eastern Ohio and western West Virginia in the 1920s. Her family's experience of daily life there is not likely to differ widely from your family's experience in similar mining communities in Kentucky. Use the information provided by your aunt-in-law to flesh out your story ("In those days, many Polish miners used to..."). But do not get sidetracked on her niece's love story. At that point, the conversation is slipping into gossip and you risk losing the focus of your interview (*but* this story of a Polish niece in love with an "American" miner may reveal nuggets about relations between immigrants and "Americans" that could additionally round out the story of your immigrant ancestors).

✐ Sometimes, a sensitive observer to an interview can provide important coaching. "John, why don't you tell about the time your mother confronted the company store manager?" or perhaps the other person will say: "But, wasn't that no later than 1937 because we were still living on Maple Street at the time and it wasn't until a month after Fred was born in January 1938 that we moved to Elm Street!"

In fact, if you know a person who might be a good coach to prod a significant but reluctant interviewee, ask that person to be present. But, again, be clear with that person about what you need. "I'll be interviewing Uncle Alec about his childhood. Would you come along to encourage him to share his information with me?"

Clear communication and thoughtful preparation of your goals for each interview will heighten your chances of success.

Exercise

✔ Identify what information is missing for you to write your lifestories.

✔ Make a list of the people who might provide this information to you. Prioritize your list according to how knowledgeable each potential interviewee is likely to be about the information you need and how "interviewable" you feel each person to be.

✔ Set up interview times. Plan ahead by asking the interviewee to bring *memory jogs*. What problems are you likely to encounter from other people? from being in the place where you will be?

✔ In what ways could other people contribute to the success of this interview? Whom might you ask?

B. At the interview

1) **Come to the interview with a list of questions.** If you prepare yourself carefully, you are more likely to leave with the information you need.

Before going out on interviews for newspaper or magazine articles, I write up the questions that I need answers to. Before the interview, I review these questions so that they are fresh in my mind. During the interview itself, however, I do not usually refer to them because I do not want interviewees to feel they are being directed toward supplying the "right" information or answer. Feeling prompted in the interview, interviewees may rechannel free-flow reminiscing into a process of outguessing the interviewer. This is clearly counterproductive.

Because I know ahead of time what information I am looking for (what work conditions were in the mills in the early 1930s, or what it was like to be a Catholic attending a public university in 1920, etc.), I can keep the interview on track. Toward the end of the session, say 15 minutes before the time I need to leave, I will check my list of questions. Usually most of them will have been answered. Sometimes, however, key topics have not yet been broached, and I will focus the remaining time on getting those questions answered. That's when I am very grateful for the list I have prepared in leisure.

2) **Be specific with the interviewee about what you are looking for**. "I want to know about the first years your parents were in this country. First, can you tell me the name of the town in Norway they came from?" (Always be thinking of memory jogs. For instance, a map of Norway could be useful. The person might say, "I don't really remember, but it was not far from Oslo. Oh, yes, there it is on the map! I remember now.")

Often, the interview is necessary to fill a specific gap in a story that you already have a lot of information on. Having an interviewee repeat information that you already know is a waste of everyone's time. *Direct the interview toward filling the gaps in your information.*

3) **Take notes during the interview**. There's nothing more frustrating and wasteful of everyone's time than returning home and not remembering significant details. At the beginning of the interview, tell interviewees that you need to record their answers and that they should not try to interpret the importance you are attributing to various bits of information by analyzing the lengths of time you spend writing them down.

If you are not comfortable writing notes, consider using a tape recorder to preserve the information for later

A tape recording of your interview can be not only a means of checking information later but a record of the person's voice-- with its intonations, accent, and modulations.

retrieval.

4) **Be wary of asking for information that can be provided by a *yes* or a *no*.** These questions are called closed-ended and they do not deepen or extend the conversation by much.

You: "Did you enjoy working on a cattle ranch?"
Interviewee: "No."

Instead of the above question that is reasonably and uselessly (to you) answered by a *no*, you might say:

You: "Tell me what you liked about working on a cattle ranch and what you didn't like".

This second example is an open-ended statement. "Tell me..." cannot be answered by a *yes* or a *no*. An open-ended statement forces the interviewee to provide additional information.

5) **Do not offer information or conclusions.** If you were to say "Those were meaningful years for you!", you *might* be putting words into the interviewee's mouth (leading her). Her answers might not then reflect what *she* is thinking-- they may simply reflect her wish not to contradict you! Instead ask "Can you tell me what conclusions you have drawn from this experience?" This allows you to know how she interprets her own experience and not how you would see it if you were her! (Haven't we all been surprised to find that another person viewed as positive what seemed to us clearly negative-- and vice versa?)

6) **Do not rush your interview.** Tolerate silences and allow time for thinking. During these silences, it is likely that your interviewee could be arriving at new definitions of his experience. Or perhaps he is simply sorting his memories for you right on the spot. All of this takes time.

Interviewees who are slow to speak could be shy or simply unused to sharing their ideas and memories. There are ways you can help ease the process. Sometimes repeating the interviewee's last words can reaffirm your deep interest. (This is not a summary statement, or an observation on your part-- it is entirely different.)

Aunt Jeanette: "Those were difficult times."
You, nodding your head in support: "Those were difficult times."

This is the antithesis of the interviewer saying, "Those were difficult times because of what you were saying

---

Videotaping can create a record of gestures, postures, general bearing, clothing, facial expressions, etc. A portable video camera can be rented quite cheaply.

"A writer is not so much someone who has something to say as he is someone who has found a process that will bring about new ideas he would not have thought of if he had not started to say them."
- William Stafford
poet

about..." Here the interviewer is planting information and could really end up quoting himself!

Another strategy for helping the conversation along is asking a question based on the interviewee's last words.

Aunt Jeanette: "Those were difficult times."

Silence.

You: "How were those times difficult?" or "Why were those times difficult for you?"

The interviewer can also simply remain calm and silent himself after the interviewee has spoken.

Aunt Jeanette: "Those were difficult times."

Silence-- even an awkwardly long one!

Aunt Jeanette, who is wondering why you are not speaking fills in the silence: "Yes, those were difficult times because..."

I have found this last "silent treatment" *very* effective in eliciting information beyond what an interviewee had originally thought to offer. To achieve this effect, however, you must decide beforehand that you will definitely not speak first and then you must wait the silence out. Sit patiently. Do not distract the interviewee with fidgeting. Silence will allow her time to synthesize, analyze, and share.

Remember: silence is sometimes the sound of someone thinking!

7) **End an interview with the question, "Do you have anything you want to add to what I have asked?"** I always do and I often find that this creates the opportunity for the interviewee to share unexpected, and potentially valuable, information.

Exercise

✔ In the previous exercise, you set up an interview. Now write a list of the questions you will need answers to during this interview.

✔ If you intend to bring your tape recorder, use it at home first to make sure you know how to operate it. Make sure you have along enough tape for the allotted time of the interview-- bring more tapes than you think you'll need.

✔ Review your questions and practice wording each one in an open-ended manner.

C. Doing academic research

Your lifestory has a larger context. This section will help you to find it.

Interviewing family members and friends will provide a personal lode of information that will greatly enhance your stories-- but interviews alone may not be enough to give your stories the depth they require.

Perhaps you already know enough about the period in which you or an ancestor lived to write about it convincingly and fully. It is more likely, however, that you have only a sketchy knowledge of the era. Your knowledge, for instance, may be based on a child's limited perspective rather than the adult's broader, more insightful one. You may know what your family had by way of household items but you may not know whether those items were commonplace in society at large or whether they reveal a special status for your family (e.g., either more comfortable or less so).

Even a minimal amount of historical research can help you place your story in a context that will round out your tale not only for your reader but for yourself. Context will help you interpret the actions and attitudes of some of your characters.

If, for instance, your ancestors came with others from Serbia and settled in a Serbian-American (-Canadian) community, their experience is vastly different from a Serbian family that found itself without co-nationals in a totally "American" or "Canadian" setting. Are the ramifications of this social history something you had thought about? If not, give it some attention because individual circumstances really do change a family's adaptation (e.g., learning a new language, intermarriage, and adopting new customs or forsaking traditions from the old country).

Here are suggestions for research:

✐ **Read about the industrialization of this continent**. Working in a sweatshop in Manhattan or a steel plant in Pittsburg is vastly different from working in an owner-run factory in a small northern New England town or on a ranch in Saskatchewan. You'll come to a different understanding of the energy it took one of your ancestors to make and carry out decisions if you understand the context in which those decisions were made.

✐ **Read about the political, religious, social climates in the old country as well as in this country.** It may be that only by understanding a larger context can you make sense of your ancestor's decisions and actions.

Even your own life has a context larger than yourself and your immediate family. Writing that "a lot of people were out of work in the first years of the 1930s" is not as clear to your readers (your grandchildren?) as writing "one in three workers in the USA was unemployed or underemployed at the beginning of the 1930s."

✐ **Read histories of the period.** They give you a more accurate sense of what was happening in the world and provide facts and dates and numbers to support your document. This research will create a framework on which to "hang" your story.

✐ **Don't forget to read old newspapers, magazines, historical society records for details on the area where you or your ancestors lived.**

If your local library does not have all the material you need to conduct your research, you can borrow through the Inter-Library Loan (ILL) program or acquire community member borrowing cards at a local university or college library. Your state, provincial, or county library is a valuable resource, too. You should inquire about these.

Exercise

✔ Go to your public library and check out a history of your ethnic, religious, or cultural group. Read it carefully, looking for both statistics and for details to use to increase the impact of your stories.

✔ Investigate a local university or college library to see if they have better materials for you to use in you research. If appropriate, obtain a community borrower's card.

✔ Find out about your state, provincial, or county library and Inter-Library Loan.

✔ Rework your stories to incorporate your research into your family or personal history.

D. Taking research notes

As you undertake library research of the kind suggested in the previous section, it will be important for you to take notes. Having information in writing will assure you that that scoundrel memory does not alter the facts. Notes will also make it easy to compare information with other material that you come across later in your research. Of course, any research is valuable only to the degree that your notes are accurate and accessible.

1) **As you take notes, write legibly and clearly**. Haven't we all had the experience of creating spontaneous "shorthand" only to discover that somehow what seemed so brilliant in the reference section of the library is absolutely meaningless now that you are at your writing desk? You scratch your head, but the information is as unavailable as if you had never taken those undecipherable notes. Write meaningfully and legibly and avoid too much spontaneous shorthand!

2) **Transcribe accurately** (and, if you are undertaking oral research, ask for spellings of *all* names, or for sources that would provide the correct spellings). This includes *all* dates, figures, and pertinent details.

Don't forget: whenever precise information is crucial to interpreting a story, verify it with additional relatives, at newspaper archives, libraries, and elsewhere. If something occurred "the year of the flood" in your town, you can check the date by going to your newspaper archives, etc.

"Those societies which cannot combine reverence for their symbols with freedom of revision must decay."
- A. N. Whitehead
philosopher

3) **Resolve discrepancies in information**. Sometimes dates or other information given to you informally will conflict with what you gather from written sources. This may be due to a simple lapse of memory on the part of your informant. If altering information does not change the story, you can simply do a correction and let it go at that --otherwise, you'll need to go back to the person and try to work through the discrepancy. Trust the written sources over the oral ones.

Discrepancies can reveal a family's (or an individual's) need to rewrite history. This will often occur in the context of *personal mythology* (See Chapter 6, Section E).

Time and personality both alter memory. The changes

that time brings to our memories are perhaps unavoidable, but the need of a personality to affirm itself is not. A person may "forget" that she was chosen to play violin in the youth orchestra at sixteen rather than at thirteen. At sixteen, this is an achievement-- yes-- but not as precocious as playing at thirteen is. This "lapse" of memory alters the personal story of the individual and transforms her from a talented person into a prodigy. In writing about this person, you will need to ask yourself why she restructured her experience. You cannot seriously continue your writing without answering that question. It is a key to understanding your story and will reveal much about this person's past and her view of life.

4) **Make notes of the sources of your information in case going back to them is necessary.** When you collect your information, you may not understand its importance or its future role in your stories. Later, while writing, you become aware that a date, a place name, or the nature of a relationship is more important than you had supposed. It may be necessary to return to your sources to amplify your notes.

There may also be discrepancies in your notes. (Did you simply copy the information incorrectly or was there an error in one of your sources? Even published books contain errors! But more likely is the possibility that you just didn't understand the meaning or significance of your information and inadvertently changed it in transcribing it.)

If this happens, you'll need to know where you got the data. Was it from an encyclopedia, a biography, or an interview? Did you gather the notes from the newspaper you read at the city library or the book at the university or the town history you found at the historical society? Always noting your sources of information could save you hours trying to retrace your steps!

Providing your readers with access to additional information for their own research into an era, a place, or an ethnic group is easy if you have kept careful notes. In doing so, you will have already compiled a bibliography for them to begin their own research. In this way, your important lifewriting project can be continued and expanded beyond your individual efforts.

E. Assuring access to your information

Having access to your information when you need it is very important. The most useful and significant information buried in a smudged scrawl in the midst of a sheaf of notes is of no use at all to you!

1) **Use 3" x 5" cards or half sheets so that each paper can clearly contain a separate bit of information.** Using large sheets may induce you to include many facts on one page-- "just so as not to waste the space". This makes it complicated to retrieve the information because you can't remember on which sheet you jotted it down.

2) **Allow for space on every page or card to jot additional information.** This can be done by leaving wide margins or by double spacing. Sometimes research or reading can uncover new facts you'll want to juxtapose with what you collected earlier. Cramming information on a sheet or writing in a tight scrawl will not make it easy for you to retrieve the material later when your writing depends on it. Give yourself a lot of space.

3) **Label each sheet to facilitate finding information.** Be as specific as you can so that it will be easy to find what you want. A recipe might get lost under the heading *kitchen*-- as might information on cookstoves under the heading *recipes*.

4) **Use ink.** Pencil marks have a way of fading and smudging. If you use felt-tip markers, be wary of any water-- raindrops, tea, tears. Water in any form smears water-based inks in no time!

5) **Write legibly so that your handwriting is discernible.** This suggestion cannot be taken too seriously! Time you save writing quickly (and most likely illegibly!) will be spent over and over again in deciphering --or having to repeat your research.

And don't forget to avoid spontaneous shorthand writing-- it will probably read like gibberish later!

F. Non-academic research

Library and archival research will create a broad context for your project, but it is not as likely to jog your own memory or uncover family details as much as other sorts of research. Your lifestories will benefit from more informal sorts of inquiry.

1) **Examine photos, both those of the family and those of the period as you find them in library books.** Compare the two. This can provide you with solid clues. Photos of your grandmother with hair coiled tightly around her head when other photos of the period show women with much looser hair styles will tell you something about her character. It may also tell you something about her social class, family background, or about her economic status-- all elements that will contribute to your understanding of yourself and your family.

Photos of you and your parents in front of the Statue of Liberty tell you that you did indeed once travel with your parents. At some point, they had enough time and disposable income to take a pleasure trip. If that disposable income, and its loss, is something you do not remember about your family, then that is an area you need to explore in an interview with a relative.

Often photos have notes on the back identifying the date and the individuals (the name of that bearded man next to Grandpa who has the same big nose you have). This information can broaden your understanding of the family context.

Photos can also suggest emotional contexts. A photo of Grandpa and Grandma sitting at opposite ends of the sofa tells you something about them that is very different from a photo of your other grandparents holding hands. This is especially true when you can back one photo with many others all providing similar clues.

Photos can reveal details that help explain unusual facts or support your intuition. Look at the background of the photos. Does it reveal material poverty or opulence? And the clothing: is it obviously home-made or does it have a tailored look? Is it new-looking, or worn-out? What is the nature of the background? Is it filled with reli-

IN LOVING MEMORY OF

𝔊edeon 𝔍. 𝔠roteau
𝔇ied 𝔐arch 10, 1967
𝔄ge 82 years

Remember, as you do any phase of lifewriting, to enjoy yourself!

gious artifacts? family photos? starkly bare? What is the function of the background objects: leisure-oriented, work-oriented, religiously-oriented?

Be a sleuth. Probe the possible meaning of the details in the photos you have on hand.

2) **Other memorabilia, besides photos, will give you precious information about your family.** Furniture, for instance, that has been handed down through the generations will tell you a lot about your people-- especially when you look at a number of pieces and compare these with furniture you see in those library books you are studying. Furniture can reveal information about social status, taste, and personality traits, especially when paired with other sources of information. Also don't forget to scrutinize what it means that this particular piece of furniture has made it down across the years: it reveals something about another person who saved *this* piece rather than *another* for posterity-- about that person's tastes, social status, self-image, etc.

The same is true of objects you yourself acquired 20 or 40 years ago. What do they tell about you at an earlier stage in your life? How have your tastes changed in the intervening years? What symbolic or emotional meaning did the purchase of that sofa or kitchen table have for you at the time?

3) **Clothing and jewelry can also reveal information as can books, diplomas, awards, tools, and personal effects (letters, diaries, poems).** In fact anything you have inherited that was bought or made can reveal clues that will help round out your research and make three-dimensional (rather than flat) characters out of the people you are writing about.

Lifestories from the Workshops:

Black Saturday by Joseph Croteau

In the twenties, everybody was making it big. Business was booming, and the stock market was going up by leaps and bounds. My father and two of his friends, Thommy Samson, a food wholesaler, and Joseph Larochelle, who owned a pharmacy and a men's clothing store, pooled their money and invested heavily in the stock-market. They would pay 10% down and make up the rest as the stocks went up in value. That was called "buying on margin": that is, their equity in securites was bought with the aid of credit obtained specifically for the purpose of buying stock.

In 1928, my father, Gédéon Croteau, bought a large new house across the street from O.B. Brown, the owner of Brown Paper Company, the only employer in Berlin, New Hampshire. The next month, Dad went down to Portland, Maine, to pick up a seven-passenger Cadillac that cost $4,000.

My father was district manager for the Metropolitan Life Insurance Company, the largest life insurance company in the world. He had just sold a large group insurance policy to the Brown Paper Company of Berlin and La Tuque, Québec.

Early in 1929, Mr. Samson decided to sell his stocks and buy the chain of twenty or thirty Nation Wide Grocery Stores in Maine and Northern New Hampshire. He made a fortune. In fact, he became a millionaire.

This story depends on a number of historical facts that enhance the essentially personal nature of the narrative.

Dad and Mr. Larochelle retained the stocks they had and kept buying more on credit.

The United States had been setting up for an economic crash for a long time. And in October 1929, the stock market collapsed. The Great Depression had begun although few people, at first, believed it could affect the entire country.

Many thought the stock market would recover in a few weeks or months. But by the end of 1929, the crash had caused losses estimated at forty billion dollars. The value of stocks on the New York Stock Exchange dropped 40%. Fortunes were wiped out. Thousands lost their jobs.

We were fortunate. As district manager, my father did not lose his job. Because he had a guaranteed salary, he was able to meet his bills. Every day, he would get a telephone call from his stockbroker to send him $1,000. Another day, it was $1,500. This went on and on until Dad's credit had been repaid. As the stocks kept dropping, he had to make up the losses. That's what happened to people who had bought stocks on margin and held on to them.

President Hoover told the people that they had no reason to fear. He called businessmen, industrialists, and labor leaders together for conferences. All these groups promised to cooperate in an effort to keep wages stable and to avoid strikes. But instead, economic conditions grew worse. By 1932, more than ten million Americans were out of work. Factories closed and banks were failing. Thousands lost their homes because they couldn't keep up their mortgage payments. Many families lived in clumps of shacks that became known as "Hoovervilles".

Joseph Croteau has three children and four grand-children. He was an insurance man for much of his working life. Since retiring, he has undertaken a number of creative hobbies including painting, drawing, gardening-- and lifewriting.

Berlin was not spared. In 1932, the Brown Paper Mill closed, and everybody in Berlin went on welfare.

Dad went to his office at 7 AM every morning and worked until late at night. People would line up in front of his office with their life insurance policies in their hands. He was authorized to give them the cash value of their policies without having to send them to the Home Office in New York, as was usually done. With the paper mill now closed, people had no other source of money. These insurance policies saved many homes from foreclosure and gave many people money to buy food.

The Republicans had little hope of winning the 1932 presidential election. They nominated Hoover and Vice-President Curtis, but did not support their candidates vigorously. The Democrats nominated Governor Franklin D. Roosevelt of New York and Speaker of the House John N. Garner of Texas, for vice-president. Roosevelt carried forty-two of the forty-eight states.

During Hoover's last four months in office, bank failures and unemployment increased. Congress paid little attention to his recommendations, and Roosevelt refused to promise support for Hoover's policies when he took office.

On Friday afternoon, March 5, 1933, the day after Roosevelt was sworn in, my father walked into the "Guaranteed" Trust Bank at 3:30 in the afternoon and deposited $250. The next morning, Roosevelt closed all the banks in the United States to stop the money panic that was spreading across the country.

My father had two houses on his hands and a mortgage in the bank that had closed that day-- Black Saturday. It never opened again.

We managed to live through it.

Chapter 5 The Truth

Lifestories from the Workshops:
My Accomplishment by Bernard H. Dion

A. What is the truth?

Telling the truth in lifewriting is not as simple a matter as it might seem at first. To begin with, by nature, truth is ultimately relative and not always evident. As lifewriters, we may repeatedly encounter the painful decision about *how much* truth to tell and *how* to tell it. In the end, the decisions we make about truth will influence our understanding of everything that has happened in our lives: the *what*, the *how*, and the *why*.

In this chapter, you will learn how to identify and to write about the various forms of truth in your lifestories.

It often comes as a surprise to lifewriters to learn from others' responses that the truth they believed to be inherent in a story is possibly a personal interpretation, one of several versions of the truth.

1) **All of your stories**, even those you presume to be true beyond any doubt, **need to be crosschecked** if your "facts" run counter to another person's remembering. This is all the more necessary if you are basing your story on these facts. Go to relatives, documents (letters, diaries, newspaper accounts, etc.), public records (birth, census, death, tax), the library, etc., in order to check your facts.

✐ **Facts are the baseline of truth.** As the temperature on a cold day can be verified by reading a thermometer, facts can also be verified by referring to authenticating sources (people, documents, records). Sometimes issues that families debate are really a matter of public record.

Part of the reward of lifewriting is setting the record straight.

Did Mother graduate from high school in 1931 or 1932? Arguing the date is a waste of time: it can be authenticated by a visit or a phone call to her high school.

Did your family live at 27 Shawmut Street from January 1935 or January 1936? The research needed to determine the true date might be as easy as bringing forward a letter dated March 1935: your mother writes about getting the last of the moving boxes unpacked! Or, you ask an elderly aunt and she says, "Your cousin Bob was born prematurely after I helped your mother and father move

Reminiscing with a parent or a sibling about family history can be an opportunity for you to deepen your relationship with that person. When your sense of the past differs, consider the discrepancy to be an opportunity for you to appreciate how you and the other person remember differently because you are different. How can you use this occasion to get to know the other person-- and yourself-- better?

boxes. He was born on January 25, 1935." Or, if your parents owned the house, you can find out when they bought it by going to the municipal registry of deeds. In fact, you can learn the entire history of the house-- when the additions were built, when the plumbing was put in, etc.

✐ **You must not bypass authenticating your information beyond reasonable doubt.** In the end, as a lifewriter, you are an historian who must have verified facts to build a solid case for your version of history.

✐ **Attribute your own versions of the truth to yourself when you cannot find the documentation to back certain "facts".** An honest, workable solution is for you to simply write "according to me, my parents lost their house in 1937 because..." and "according to my sister Edna (or brother Edgar), they lost it because..."

2) **Other "facts" in your lifestories may be easy to evaluate as improbable or impossible because logical sequencing of events contradicts them.** For instance, your daughter was born in 1948; she cannot possibly remember how much she loved sleeping at your parents' apartment on Shawmut Street from which your parents moved in 1947! Your cousin Fred who was killed in Normandy on D-Day in 1944 could not possibly have swindled your grandparents out of their savings in 1945 when they were persuaded to invest in phoney stocks!

Stories like the cousin Fred one can survive in a family and become the documentation people use as back up when they talk of Fred's sleazy character-- after all didn't he swindle your grandparents in 1945!

3) **Learn to distinguish between truth that is relevant and truth that is irrelevant.** Digging too deeply can sometimes be a waste of time.

For example, do you really need to authenticate whether it was John or James, when you were four, who pushed you off the swing? You suffered a concussion when the seat of the swing hit your head. John says it was James; James says it was John. After fifty years, a fog has rolled over your family's collective memory. You have no wish to carry out a vendetta against either of your brothers. At this point, beyond idle curiosity, who pushed you is fairly irrelevant. What is crucial is the head injury you suffered. You need to write about your concussion, not about the irrelevant matter of who pushed you. In this instance, you can write: "According to John, James did it and, according to James, John was the culprit. At any rate, I was hospitalized with..." More truth than that is simply immaterial and nit-picky. It is not worth pursuing.

4) **Attribute to someone's opinion what cannot be authenticated.** Whenever you decide that pursuing the truth is irrelevant or impossible (e.g., events occurred a long time ago and everyone involved is now gone), you must embed the opinion in a phrase that makes it clear whose it is. Use phrases like "My brother Francis believes that...", "My mother always said that...", "According to me...",

Do challenge your memory by checking out the facts to the extent possible and practicable. When no clear verifiable truth emerges, **remember your ultimate goal is recording *your version* of the truth-- not someone else's.**

An older child may remember poor, youthful parents full of energy for playing with them. A younger child may remember financially secure but older parents who did not tussle on the living room rug.

Exercise

Reread what you have written so far for the accuracy of its truth.

✔ Distinguish between the *relevant* truths in your stories and the *irrelevant* truths.

✔ Are you absolutely sure of the accuracy of all your relevant truths? Would everyone in your family, for instance, agree to your "facts" (vs. interpretation, which is not in question here)?

✔ Make a list of resources (relatives, letters, newspapers, etc.) to authenticate material.

✔ If, while you are crosschecking your information, you uncover discrepancies in versions of the truth, authenticate a likely version of the truth. If you cannot, acknowledge that the version you have included is unauthenticated by introducing it with a phrase like "According to me,..." or "It would seem to me that..." or "My guess is..."

B. Some self-evident truths

Once you have verified all the facts that can or need to

In this section, you will learn how to expand the text of your lifestories by learning how to make an "educated guess" or reasonable inference.

"The artist 'lies' in order to reach another kind of truth."
- Pablo Picasso
artist

be verified, other truths may become evident. But these truths may not be the sort you can authenticate.

For instance, your parents were married in 1930. Most young couples are without solid financial backing. Your parents, as much as you and anyone else knows, didn't have any "rich uncle" to ease them through these first years. Are you justified in concluding that they must have felt the negative effects of the Depression during their first days together?

You can't "prove" this, of course. If, as scientists do with their theories, you proceeded as if your hypothesis were true-- that your parents must have had a lean time at first, what insights does that provide you about decisions they made during those years, about decisions they made in their later life together? Educated guesses like this, based on *reasonable inferences*, can make another person's life more understandable and your portrait more full.

As you include your interpretations, always attribute them to yourself by attaching phrases like "It seems to me that..." and "If that were true, then..." Your interpretation, or perhaps it is an inference, will take its place as a *possible truth* in the story you are writing. Although it is essentially different from verifiable truth, *the inferred truth has a rightful place in your writing*. Without it, your story will be poorer.

Exercise:

Look at the material you have gathered or at the stories you have written.

✔ How will making inferences change or affect these stories? (Important: if you choose to make inferences, remember to place them in the context of a phrase like "I would think that..." or "We can suppose that...")

✔ Have you made all inferences possible to extend your stories? If you haven't, try including at least one to help your reader interpret your characters or story. Remember to "own" your inferences and attribute them to yourself or to the person who made them.

C. Using your intuition

There is another sort of truth that is neither verifiable, nor is it an educated guess. This truth is intuitive.

"Mother never liked living at 27 Shawmut Street" is an example of intuitive truth. No matter what others may say, and your sister Edna is convinced of the opposite, you have a "gut" feeling that your perception of your mother's unhappiness is correct.

If your mother is no longer alive, authenticating your "gut" feeling may be impossible-- and even if she is, your mother may be unable, for many reasons, to admit to the truth. (See the following section of this chapter: *How much truth should you tell?*)

As in the example on the previous page in which you were exhorted to proceed as a scientist does-- on a hypothesis-- ask yourself if your "gut" feeling helps to explain other things. Does it, for instance, explain behavior and attitudes that might otherwise be attributable only to a failing in your mother's character?

As you apply this "test", it may become obvious that your "gut" feeling explains a lot of things that happened in your family. How will you write about intuitive truths? They are not only unprovable but they may also, in your family, be the subject of disagreement.

My suggestion is: state your intuition and say why it seems right. Then give the points of view of other people equal space. Your family readers need and deserve these different interpretations-- especially if there is no way to authenticate which is true-- or nearer being true.

At the workshops

After Helen had finished reading her account, a story of going to a lakeside camp for part of the summer when she was 10, she closed her notebook and looked around the room, waiting for our response.

Like others around the long table, I sat not saying anything. There was something missing to her story. It simply didn't feel right. My intuition was that Helen was not telling the truth. She had somehow reconstituted events to hide the truth about someone or something. Did she know what she had done?

"Who wants to share what you liked about the piece?" I asked, but no one answered. At the workshop table, the men and the women seemed as reluctant as I to open the discussion.

People have a sense about when they're being told a "tall tale". That day was no exception. I waited. Helen waited. The workshoppers waited.

Then, from across the table, Linette, a woman in her sixties, shook her head and said, "I don't think that's the way it happened."

We gasped. How would Helen accept this intuitive response?

Helen looked up. "As a matter of fact, it didn't happen that way! I didn't want to write about the way it happened."

The others seemed uneasy. No one spoke.

I said, "You don't have to tell us what really happened, but you do need to know that you can't not tell the truth and expect us not to notice."

Softly one woman to Helen's side added, "You can keep the truth from us, but you haven't fooled us. What's important is that you haven't kept the truth from yourself. I hope you've been honest with yourself about what happened."

Then, Helen spoke to us about why she had changed her story, about the pain and the fear of that summer when she was 10.

She seemed relieved that we had intuited the truth.

Exercise:

✔ Write about an incident in your life in a way that your intuition tells you is true.

✔ Include in your stories whenever possible intuitive interpretations that vary with each other and attribute them to the specific individuals who made them.

D. How much truth should you tell?

You have a right to maintain the boundaries you are comfortable with.

There is another dilemma to face when you are dealing with the truth. *How much* of it do you have to tell to tell the truth? At what point does withholding the truth become a lie? For instance, in all her diaries, as Anaïs Nin celebrated the freedoms of her life as an artist, she never once mentioned that she was being bankrolled by a husband. True, she could not mention his name or details of his life because he had refused her legal permission to do so, but wouldn't it have been more truthful to have alluded to the fact that there was a working-everyday husband who was paying the bills and whom she could not describe more than that?   In that sense, her diaries have always seemed to me to contain a fundamental lie.

How much truth to tell is a sensitive decision that can be made only in the context of the writer's life and family. The following are considerations to keep in mind when deciding how to solve your "truth problems".

1) **Withholding information can significantly alter your reader's interpretation of a story.** You risk a lie whenever you decide to keep a part of the truth hidden.

2) **Conversely, writing memoirs is not the opportunity to tell everything!** Nor is it the time to impose your version of an ugly scene and get your revenge on the people who are not available to defend themselves.

In a conversation, when someone tries to engage you on his side, *don't you feel that your good will is being abused?* Your readers will feel abused, too, if your goal is to enlist them *against* someone else. Your readers are looking for insight-- not partisanship! You may force them to stop reading your story in order to protect their integrity.

3) **You do not have to tell something you do not feel comfortable telling.** You have the right to your privacy and do not have to divulge details you do not want to share.

Yes, definitely, a case can be built around the fact that withholding information is a form of lying (see #1 above). A case can also be built around your need to protect yourself! You are not an exhibitionist nor a masochist. *Relationships and your dignity as a person are sometimes more important than the truth.* This is *your* decision. Like Helen (p. 99), be aware of having the choice-- and don't ever hide the truth from yourself even if you choose not to share it with others.

4) **Be wary of recording someone else's views of your life or of the lives of others in your family.** For example, within a family, stories sometimes acquire the status of an "official" version. These "official" stories are often initiated by the *dominant* parent (the one who makes the rules in the

Don't worry about making your prose beautiful. Instead reach for truth. "Tell it like it was!" Hemingway wrote about writing "true sentences". It is all you can aspire to. With truth, as Keats wrote, comes beauty.

"I want to keep some things private. My children don't have to know everything about me!"
     - Workshop writer

family). These stories serve as "propaganda" for that parent's point of view (see *At the workshops* below). Evidence of this is how the *less dominant* parent is usually evaluated on the criteria set by the dominant one. Writing beyond this "propaganda" about the less dominant parent (or the not-of-the-same-mold sibling) can be one of the major problems lifewriters face. This challenge must not be underrated. Deal with it courageously.

*Be a sleuth. Go beyond (or beneath) the apparent story to get at the **real** story. Be honest with yourself-- and write the story your intuition tells you is true.*

At the workshops

Nancy wrote about her father. In her family, it was always said that he was a bit shiftless and that he had no ambition. As Nancy delved into her father's life, however, "walking a while in his shoes", she grew to have a different interpretation of his life's journey-- but it was not easy for her to give up the official family version.

The facts did bear out that her father had gone from one job to another but she uncovered a reason for this she had hidden from herself all her life. Her father had shown a dedication to music, a longstanding participation in church and community music groups, an advocacy of music education in the schools, a patient collection of a music library. She had never seen any relationship between his love for music and his lack of job ambition, but now it began to make sense.

Her father had passed up a promotion at work in 1947. This had been an important piece of evidence in the family's (mostly the mother's) documentation of the father's shiftlessness. But Nancy now realized that the promotion would have required that her father work evenings. He would have had to forfeit directing the choral group he had been working with since 1946 (this is an example of how accurate dating can be crucial to interpreting family history!).

As Nancy continued examining her father's life, she realized that her mother's allegations of her father's shiftlessness and lack of steadfastness were not necessarily true either. To the contrary, her father had shown an admirable ability to meet basic family responsibilities while nurturing his gift for music, the great passion of his life. The emotional reinforcement of work was secondary to him.

Her mother had not prized the emotional rewards of music in her husband's life as highly as she regretted the loss of increased pay and a husband's job status in her own. In the mother's version of the truth, she had suffered many difficulties because of the father's "character flaw". She insisted she was to be praised for what she had had to endure. Poor

Mother!

Nancy realized she had been taught to view her father's life through a wife's eyes, not a daughter's! Now she began to wonder what might have been had her mother supported his efforts to develop his talents rather than driven them under. Might her father have worked out a way to support the family with his work in music?

Determined now to write as a daughter, Nancy nonetheless felt herself pitted against her mother and her mother's different interpretation of the man on whom she depended for status.

Initially, despite what she felt to be the truth, her conditioning was still strong, and she could not reveal what she now saw as the truth. It is what she had done all her life; what had been expected by her mother. She felt it would be disloyal to her mother to tell a different truth.

In the end, however, Nancy had to accept that the view she had held was not her own point of view but her mother's. As an adult, she was now free to see her father as he might have been. Through the work of lifewriting, she was empowered to say to her mother, "I love you and I do not see my father as you saw him."

Exercise

✔ Identify an "official" family story that makes you uncomfortable.

✔ Write your own version of this story. Use as many details as you can remember. Don't forget to make "educated guesses". (Remember: you do not have to share your writing with anyone! You can even throw it away once you have written it!)

✔ How do you feel now to have told a truth that you were uncomfortable about? Do you feel you can include this story in the final version of your lifestory? What will you do about the other version of the truth-- the one that may have been propaganda for someone else's point of view?

✔ Do you know who might be responsible for this version? What is your feeling now for, and your evaluation of, this person? It is important for you to understand *why* the person fostered and allowed this official version to circulate.

E. How do you tell the truth?

Other issues arise, not around *what* the truth is, but *how* the truth is told.

We all love well-told stories. We love the entertainment, the effects, of a good plot built around solid characterization. As we share stories in our everyday conversations, we inevitably use many fiction elements. When we say "And then she said...", we are using dialogue-- it's a fiction technique.

In telling the truth, we will often veer toward using fiction techniques. In fact, we don't seem to need urging at all to adapt fiction methods to our stories-- we do it spontaneously.

Many people ask, "But, am I twisting things when I use fiction techniques?"

✐ *Should a writer invent dialogue between his characters?* He does not, after all, have a tape recording of the conversations of the people he is writing about.

✐ *Can the writer ascribe articles of clothing to an individual when he can't be sure that that individual wore such an article on a specific day?*

✐ *How does a writer share with his reader the thoughts that he suspects an individual might have had?* After all, he was not in that person's head!

Different individuals arrive at different solutions. Here are some choices available to lifewriters who feel a conflict in ascribing dialogue or other details to their stories.

1) **Write an introduction or preface to your lifestory.** Mention that you are using fiction techniques when you ascribe specific conversations and reactions to an individual. In this way, you attest that each of these elements are, to the best of your knowledge, *representative* of what the character might have said or worn or done. You might write that the person's speech is in keeping with how the person might have spoken, and in a tone the person would have been comfortable with. As to clothing, you might write that you wish to give a sense of the total person and are sharing information about the character and inserting

this information in such a way as to be unobtrusive, but the reader should not infer that all the pairings of clothing and times are accurate.

2) **Use indirect discourse (a statement introduced by using or implying the word *that*).** Here's an indirect discourse: "My grandmother said (that) she would not leave". A direct discourse would be: "My grandmother said, 'I will not leave' ". Notice, too, that the first example does not use quotation marks while the second does.

In the same vein, you might mention: "My grandmother had a red dress and perhaps she was wearing it that day." In this way, you are not introducing misinformation but your story is somewhat less immediate. You will always sacrifice immediacy and impact with this technique, but you gain truthfulness when you use indirect methods. Indirect discourse is a less attractive method to me than direct quotes because of this loss of impact but it is a perfectly acceptable choice of method to use.

3) **Never use dialogue or make a reference that is not authenticated.** This choice can be very limiting in terms of storytelling. The characters never actually say *anything* in their own voices; they never appear with particular hair styles or pieces of clothing. They probably won't ever do things like look out of windows either or wish they had not said something, or eat a meal-- all fictional details that will make your characters come alive in your lifestories.

Without fiction techniques, your story will have aspects of hearsay rather than the you-were-there immediacy of storytelling at its best. But, if using no fiction techniques is your choice, you will have told your story in the way you want to tell it. That is very important!

Exercise

✔ If you have not already used dialogue to portray truth, try introducing some into one of your stories. Keep the dialogue to no more than two or three exchanges. (Long dialogue is more difficult to write.)

✔ A good spot for dialogue is as a replacement for adjectives. An adjective such as *angry*

("I will never, never allow you to do that--ever!") or *generous* ("Take these seedlings and if you need more come back. I could perhaps spare a few more") can easily be translated into dialogue.

✔ Try introducing a character's clothing, gestures, and thoughts into your writing.

Lifestories from the Workshops:

My Accomplishment *by Bernard H. Dion*

This is a story which tells the unpleasant truth of a boy's relationship with his father. The writer tells the truth without bitterness and without making the reader uncomfortable.

I never had a bicycle. My cousin Ray, who was an only child, had one: a brand-new, shiny, green-and-white 26" Columbia. He had everything, and all of us kids envied him.

It was summertime, and I was making a daily trip to the dump in my hometown of Swansea, Massachusetts because I had promised myself that, before school started again in September, I'd have myself a bike, too. These trips netted me a back wheel in worse shape than a front one whose spokes were missing-- there were no guts in the hub, even fewer spokes and it was crooked besides. Before long, I found handlebars, a rear fender, a rear carrier, and two tires that were of no use to the person who had thrown them out, but to me they were good enough to at least get my bike on the road.

Soon I had a 28" frame, a fork, and a bare seat that could easily be done over with a rabbit skin, a post without its handlebars, and a sprocket assembly.

I was sitting on the back steps one day with all these parts around me when my father came home from work. He approached me with a quizzical look on his face that said, "Good grief, now what?" With pain in his voice, he managed to say "What's all this junk, and where'd it come from?"

"It came from the dump, Pa," I said, "and it's gonna be a bike."

"A bike?" my father grunted as he shook his head and went into the house. Over his shoulder, he said, "Spending so much time at the dump-- it'll kill you one of these days! You'll catch some awful disease from all that filth".

With my father's tools, I was able to straighten out the fork and the frame and I sanded everything right down to the metal so I had some respectable-looking parts ready for assembly. Somewhere, somehow, though, I had to get some spokes, three sets of bearings, a front fender, a chain, and some paint. I couldn't possibly buy all these things because I was looking at a dollar and a half here, and in the mid '30s money like that didn't come easy.

There was no point in going to my father for money to help me put a lot of junk together-- he'd already voiced his opinion with a grunt. I had a paper route, but that money went to my mother. I had to get some money that only I knew about. How could I do it? Soda bottles and milk bottles-- that's how!

My paper customers often tipped me by giving me bottles that my mother never knew about. I would always cash them in before I got home and buy candy and penny cigarettes from Moe, who owned the only drugstore in town. Now I saved the money for the missing parts I needed.

Born in Fall River, Massachusetts, Bernard H. Dion is the father of five daughters. For many years, he worked as a credit union manager. He enjoys playing golf and cribbage and keeping abreast of politics.

Finally, after cashing in many bottles and doing much swapping with Bob Nadeau, who lived next door, I finished my bicycle. I painted it green and even striped the fenders and post in white. I was ready to show my father what I'd accomplished.

Sitting on the back steps, with my shiny green and white bike leaning against the foundation, I waited for my father to come home from work. I was proud of my summer's accomplishment and I knew he would be proud of me, too. At last, his car turned into the driveway, and he saw me sitting there. He saw the bike, too, because he looked and then hesitated for a moment as if to think of some complimentary remark. But as he walked up to me he looked at my bicycle with displeasure.

"I'm telling you for the last time, I don't want you borrowing expensive things like a bicycle from your friends! If you break it, you'll be in all kinds of trouble!"

And with that he walked into the house.

Chapter 6 More than "Just the Facts, Ma'am!"

A.   Writing the basic **what**

B.   Going beyond **what** to **how** and **why**

C.   **Theme**: it's the life of your stories.

D.   Inherited themes

E.   Personal myths

F.   Don't preach to me!

G.   The glazed-over-eyes test

Lifestories from the Workshops:
Little Did I Know by Trudy Laliberté

A. Writing the basic *what*

Dates and facts are necessary to lifewriting in the same way route numbers are necessary to maps. It's not only that dates and facts provide interesting information but that they keep you and your readers on the right road as you make your way through your lifestory.

The dates and facts you want to include in your lifestories can be written up in a variety of ways.

1) **You can write a chronology.** A chronology is a **simple** narrative of dates and facts. As entry level lifewriting, a chronology is important in conserving family history because it records dates and facts for your readers (i.e. Grandma and Grandpa bought a farm in Washington, Missouri, in the spring of 1932. They planted a large market garden; in June of the same year, they added three cows and two pigs to their venture).

✐ *A chronology leaves out big pieces of information that are neither dates nor facts.* It does not tell your readers *why* your grandparents moved to the farm or *how* they felt about being there. Your readers will wonder about whether they had an easy or a difficult time of farming. Did the experience help them to grow personally? Was it a good decision on their part? Remember that *guidance* and *reassurance* are important functions of storytelling.

To provide answers to these questions, you must write more than a chronology.

2) **You can add action to your chronology.** *This will make your stories easier to understand and more interesting to read.* You are introducing action when you place events (and the dates and facts that surround them) into a cause and effect relationship. "Because the drought grew worse week by week that summer (*cause*), Grandpa and Grandma hauled water every evening to the gardens (*effect*)." Another word for the action of a story is *plot*.

3) **You can heighten the impact of your action-en-**

This chapter will help you to write both the surface and the depth of your stories. It will help you understand what made the life you are writing about so unique and interesting.

hanced chronology with *suspense*. Suspense emphasizes the *effects* which the *causes* you write about are likely to have on your characters. It suggests the consequences they do not yet foresee but which will, as you know, play a role in their lives.

With the addition of action, especially of suspenseful action, what might have started out as a chronology is now fleshed out and your readers are more likely to be intrigued and concerned as they read your story. "Day after day the sky was clear without any clouds. The gardens were very dry. Grandpa and Grandma wondered about what they would do if the crops failed. All over the United States jobs were being eliminated as the Depression deepened. Would there be any job for Grandpa away from the farm to help tide them over-- or would they simply have to forfeit their land and join the ranks of the urban poor?"

Generally speaking, the action, or plot, of a story will provide the interest to keep your audience reading-- especially if it contains suspense. Action is the framework on which *characterization*, *setting* (Chapter 3), and *theme* (see Section C below) are built.

Enhanced by action and suspense, your story is now more entertaining than it was as a chronology. There is still an element missing however. Without telling the *why* of your story, you will fail to satisfy your readers' curiosity about the characters you present.

B. Going beyond *what* to *why* and *how*

This section explores how to uncover the inner meaning of your life.

Why do basic facts in one person's life sometimes resemble those in another's and yet produce such different effects? Frequently it is not so much *what* we do that touches, and changes, our lives as *why* and *how* we do it. The intentions behind our actions as well as the manner in which we act are often more impactful than the actions themselves. To be successful in conveying the essence of your life, write about the *why* and the *how* as well as the *what*.

1) **Add interpretation to your chronology and plot**. Tell *why* and *how* your grandparents persevered in this difficult work (perhaps something about their belief in working for themselves and in how working together would deepen their relationship, or perhaps about their certainty that life was meant to be hard in this way).

Consider the following: "Because the drought grew worse week by week that summer of 1932, Grandpa and Grandma hauled water every evening to the gardens. They had invested all they owned in the farm which they had dreamed of buying for years. If it failed, they would be forced to go back to the city to live on the dole. Both Grandma and Grandpa were go-getters. Losing not only their livelihood but also their source of meaningful activity was unthinkable for them."

In the example above, the necessary facts and dates *as well as* plot (even if a slight one) are joined by something more: *insight* into *why* and *how*. Your readers will know your grandparents better than they would by reading a mere chronology or a simple action story. You have added motivation, the *why* that lends meaning to your story, and the *how* that shows your grandparents' unique style.

2) **Look inside and around you to uncover the why and the how of your stories**. To write the previous example, you might have recalled statements your grandparents themselves made in their conversations, statements in which the why and the how may be very clear. Your parents knew things about your grandparents that you didn't. Look to answers for your how and why questions in the stories they told you when you were a child. If they are still alive, interview them about your grandparents. You might ask other relatives, too, for their versions of the deeper answers. In looking for insights, do not overlook your intuition; do visualization; use a combination of all the above (see Chapter 2, Section D-- *Memory Jogs*).

3) **Avoid writing without insight into the *why* or the *how***. *Without these, your writing will not be satisfying for you or your readers.* Most stories on TV are proof of this. They are well-plotted, but they offer no insight into the motiva-

tions of their characters other than what is necessary to wrap up the plot in the half-hour slot. Because these TV stories depend entirely on action rather than on well-rounded characters with internal motivation, TV characters can be called "stick " characters-- portraits about as interesting as the one dimensional "stick" figures drawn by children and adults without much drawing ability.

These well-plotted TV stories leave thoughtful viewers unsatisfied, feeling they've wasted their time. How long can stick characters hold anyone's interest? Such vacuous stories demonstrate, once again, the importance of writing not only the *what* but the *why* and the *how* of an action.

Exercise

✔ Record the plots of several TV shows.

✔ Which were stuck at the *chronology* stage?

✔ How did they make use of *suspense*? Was suspense enough? How so?

✔ To what degree did each program depend on *action* that did not require the *inner motivation* of the character: the blond fluffhead was similar to the dark-haired fluffhead on another program; the dark, strong-but-silent type of one show could have been substituted for the blond, strong-but-silent type from another?

✔ To what degree did each program attempt to show a character that was truly individualized (that could not be substituted for any other)?

✔ Do you find the "fleshed out" characters more satisfying? Why?

C. *Theme: it's the life of your stories.*

Underlying all of your writing is its **theme**. The theme is really a message, the global way in which you understand your story-- either in its entirety or in its parts. The theme conveys the essence of the *you* (or the *them*) that you want the reader, and history, to know and understand. The theme provides spirit to your piece, the breath of life that individualizes your story.

All writing has theme or message. Theme can be superficial or deep. Sometimes you can recapitulate it in one word (e.g., perseverance). At other times, you need a phrase or a sentence (e.g., what happens to us in our lives is always part of our journey and not separate from it). Even the superficial, all-plot TV program has a theme, but it is likely to be something as shallow as "we're the 'good' guys and they're the 'bad' guys" or as insidious (and hidden) as "materialism brings happiness".

1) **The theme is dependent on your insights.** Insights, as I mentioned in the previous section, are glimpses of understanding. ("Oh, *that's* why-- or how-- she must have done that!") As you view your stories over time, your insights will accumulate. When you bring them into ever sharper focus, you begin to see larger, broader conclusions about the life you are writing about-- and even the meaning of life itself. The themes of your stories evolve from, and are synonymous with, these conclusions.

✐ **Self-serving excuses should not be confused with insight.** For instance, we might write in our lifestories that it was because of our parents' style of raising children or of the strictures of our ethnic group or of the limitations imposed by our socio-economic class that we have not achieved certain goals. Of course, this "insight" fails to account for our failure as adults to create our own opportunities to overcome these very real shortcomings or to turn them into advantages in a creative way. This "insight", then, is really a self-serving excuse to avoid doing work on how we live our lives.

2) **Theme influences choices for every element in a story: plot development, characterization, and setting.** Let's look at these elements. Here's the shell of the plot: your father was laid off; a difficult time followed for the family; your father received additional training and obtained a different job.

Your treatment of this plot will vary according to your theme. Let's suppose the following is your theme: "events

In this section, you will look at the message you are giving your reader in your stories.

"I had no idea I was revealing so much about myself through my writing."
   - Workshop writer

whose consequences we can't understand happen gratu-itously to us in our lives, but we can always make the best of things." In the elaboration of this particular theme (message), you will find it natural to pair your father's be-ing laid off not only with his reaction at the time but also with its consequences. Because of your positive theme, you will write about the new circumstances that developed for your father and about his psychological growth (character). To develop your theme, you will show how important it was for him to "roll with the punches", to al-low himself to experience being without the identity his job and his role as family provider had furnished, and ulti-mately to exercise choices that led to new, satisfying pur-suits.

Our choices of themes tell us a lot about how we view life. Our awareness of that can provide us with an opportunity for emotional growth as we write-- and as we live.

So much for one plot development. Now imagine that your theme (obviously based on different insights) is: "life deals each of us gratuitous, unwarranted dirty tricks and my father was no exception". In this story, you would em-phasize the role other people played in your father's being laid off and how no one helped him. You would dwell on the negative elements-- how the economic demands made on him by his children left him with few choices, how his insufficient education (due in turn to his parents, his ethnic group, etc.) limited his job options. You would probably undervalue the training that led to a different job and fail to acknowledge the psychological growth he experienced as a result of it and his new job challenges.

Both of these plot developments are based on the same facts, but the stories themselves are very different because they are in-spired by very different themes. As a writer, you must be aware that your theme (the message you impart) affects every fact in your story. By conscious choice and use of theme, you can make your story into a distinct and unique account.

3) **Discover the theme of your story as you proceed. It is all right to begin writing without a specific theme in mind.** As you write and re-write (re-writing is crucial in deepening your sense of meaning), be attentive to the theme which may gradually reveal itself to you. This pro-cess can be an intriguing one if you are open to it. Theme is revealed as you find yourself using certain words or ex-pressing certain ideas over and over again. Discovering

your theme in this way is not only important but it can catch your interest and make your lifewriting more compelling. It will keep you coming back to your writing table.

Exercise

Look at the stories you have written so far and examine them for theme.

✔ What are your stories saying beyond the facts? Finish this sentence for each of several of your stories: "This story shows how it is important for people to..."

✔ Are you gearing your *theme* (message) to an intended audience (i.e., grandchildren)? How has this influenced your plot development, your characterization, and your use of setting?

✔ What have you discovered about your theme while writing? Has the theme changed? How has this affected your interest?

D. Inherited themes

As you articulate your theme (whether you set out with a sense of it or discover it as you proceed), ask yourself if this theme is *really* yours-- does it reflect your present understanding of life's workings? Or is it is a residue of the accepted "wisdom" of someone else: a parent, another adult figure, society at large?

1) **Writers who recognize, acknowledge, and explore their own themes in their writing are more apt to present us with clear to-the-point stories than those who repeat inherited themes.**

Early in our lives, you and I were naturally and rightfully the recipients of someone else's-- a parent's or grandparent's-- understanding and interpretation of life. As long as these interpretations correspond to our own adult views, we can write easily within their context. What happens often, however, is that we continue to espouse an-

In this section, you will learn to identify the themes you received from others as part of your acculturation into your family, ethnic group, or other culture.

other person's point of view without realizing that it has ceased to be our own. When challenged, we will say "Well, I guess I really don't believe that anymore. Isn't it something how I wrote (or said) that!"

✐ **If you write from someone else's differing point of view-- consciously or unconsciously, your writing will reveal the conflict between this other point of view and yours.** Your readers will sense that you are writing someone else's themes rather than your own. They will be uncomfortable with your story and may tend to dismiss it.

If you want to be taken seriously as a lifewriter, it comes down to being "in charge". *This is your story.* You don't have to let someone else's perception dictate what you will write-- although it is often useful and honest to tell the reader how another person understood an experience or relationship differently. Elsewhere in this book, I have often suggested that you include varying and even opposing accounts in your lifestories and that you attribute these accounts to the other people who expressed them. You can do so by using a phrase like "This is Irving's version of what happened..." Doing this, you will not be writing from anyone's point of view but your own.

✐ **Championing someone else's themes is a major source of "writer's block".** The natural way to see things is through your own point of view. The unconscious quickly refuses to provide inspiration to writers who subvert this natural relationship to life when they uphold someone else's point of view rather than their own. The result of this boycott by the unconscious is the proverbial "writer's block". Sometimes a "writer's block" is a way the unconscious has of telling us that we are not paying enough attention to our own insights. Next time you are stumped with your writing, ask yourself if you are being entirely honest in your lifestories.

2) **When you distort your insights in order not to contradict other people's themes, you are also setting your readers up to dismiss what you write.** They will know that your interpretation is not the product of insight but just another instance of family "whitewashing". For instance, if you are driven (by your loyalty to a family theme) to depict a character as always fighting for goodness and justice, a true "heroine", but in your heart you ex-

"I wanted to write about a family feud, but I went blank. All I could think of was how my mother, who's been gone for 23 years, always wanted us to be close."
- Workshop writer

perienced her as occasionally questionable in her ethics, your readers will pick this up intuitively. Just as when you write entirely from someone else's point of view, distorting your point of view will lead your readers to distrust your writing both here and elsewhere (and possibly everywhere).

At the workshops

Ursula wrote of a brother, nine years her senior. While babysitting her, he put castor oil in a drink he offered to her as a reward. Her subsequent diarrhea was predictable and her ensuing trips to the bathroom became a family joke, told repeatedly when members got together over the years.

As she read her story, Ursula laughed at that evening of running to the toilet sixty years earlier. "What a joker he was," she said, repeating the story as if it had happened to someone else. The piece was well-written stylistically, but it lacked conviction.

Ursula asked for our reactions. Participants were restrained. Were they being polite (it was, after all, only our second meeting and people didn't know each other well) or had they simply not sensed anything wrong here?

As leader, I had to assure the success of future discussions, so I said, "I need to know about why your brother had your family's permission to put castor oil in your drink."

She said she didn't know what I meant. He certainly didn't have anyone's permission to give her castor oil!

I pointed out that, in my birth family and in my own nuclear family, a child would have absolute prohibition against behaving as her brother had. An inner censor would have stopped me as a child and would stop my own children from doing what frankly seemed abusive. We talked then about family cultures and what they do or do not foster according to permissions they tacitly bestow.

Ursula's mother, it turned out, was a widow who indulged her fifteen-year-old son and set few limits for him. Her mother seemed to have been confused. Rather than discipline the boy, Ursula admitted, her mother had often given in to him. Perhaps her brother was testing limits to find out if she would respond to him in a parental role?

He was certainly right that he could get away with doing what he had done. Hadn't Ursula herself laughed as she told the story-- revealing that she had also given permission to have this trick played on her? Why was it ok to put castor oil in the glass of a six year old? Would it have been ok to do it to anyone else in the family? What other tricks were ok? with whom?

The brother, we learned, had left home while still young and, after that, had had little to do with anyone in the family.

A number of sessions later, on assignment to rewrite an earlier story into a more polished version, Ursula reworked her castor oil story. Now, however, when she read her story, she no longer laughed. The story had ceased to be a funny one for her. In fact, there had appeared a note of anger-- but she was not angry at her brother. He was acting out. No, now, she was angry at her mother! Where had she been during those years? Why had she not set limits for the older brother as a mother should? Why had her mother not protected her then and at other times?

Ursula had experienced her mother's laissez faire *as abandonment. As she had rewritten her story, it had become a much larger one-- and a much better one, too, because it was her own version of the castor oil episode. She was now freed of having to repeat the official family story that had made her the fall guy for her brother's abuse and her mother's neglect. In this official version, her mother had no responsibility for her son's behavior.*

The group, now in its final weeks of being together, admitted they had been uncomfortable with her earlier version. Ursula smiled with relief. Although she was now in her late sixties, the little girl in her had been afraid of being ridiculed for delivering this new, altered account.

Ursula referred to this story several times in remaining sessions. Re-working this story had provided her with a valuable insight into her family and her life.

Exercise

Write about a theme in your life that you have had difficulty accepting as your own.

✔ As a first step, write a story about how another point of view was imposed on you. This is often something that one of your parents (or teacher or clergyman) said repeatedly about you, or did to or for you, that constricted your development or that was not true for you. Often, this sort of intervention was very confusing. Unable to contradict authority figures, we accept their misinterpretation of us as "truth". Children can thus come to believe themselves to be stupid, incapable, unattractive, or worse.

✔ Write about how long you believed this message and its effects on you.

✔ Now, write about the experience that changed your understanding. How did you grow to know who you were and to view life from your own point of view ("I'm not stupid or ugly or superfluous!")? Did a new school or job or love affair contradict the negative view you had accepted? What role did the old message play in maintaining the status quo of its context?

E. Personal Myths

No life can be understood separately from its myths. A myth is not a fantastical made-up story nor is it, as the word is commonly used, a synonym for a "lie" or erroneous belief ("three myths about losing weight!").

Myths are the story forms of how we perceive the world and life. How we live our lives is determined by our myths but our lives also reveal our myths to ourselves and to the world.

According to the Swiss psychoanalyst, Carl Jung, dominant psychic forces which he called **archetypes** (instincts or patterns of thought) have a powerful role in our lives. Just as migratory birds have an instinct to fly north and south at appropriate times, we also are said to have a form of character instinct (called *archetypes*) that governs many of our actions and reactions. These archetypes determine the contents of the personal myths by which we live our lives.

Throughout our lives, these archetypes have an influence on us-- positive, negative, and sometimes alternately one and then the other. As we write about ourselves or other people, we need to assess archetypes and how we were able to capitalize on or compensate for them.

The following are only a few examples (the martyr, the orphan, and the prince-left-at-the-pauper's-door) to help you understand the role of personal myths. There are many more archetypes and, if you find you are interested in learning more about this topic, read some of the books available on the subject. (See Appendix B for a reading list.)

A) *People who are "giving" people can be said to be "martyrs".* They are the ones who volunteer and take on extra tasks. As such, they are instrumental in the life of a community and get much of its work done. Martin Luther King, Salvador Allende, and Mother Theresa are well-known and praiseworthy examples of the martyr archetype. Society often clearly benefits from the sacrifices of martyrs who, pushed to their limits, are moved to give even their own lives for the higher good of the community

This section helps you to incorporate personal myths into your writing.

The warrior is always fighting city hall.

at large.

On the negative side of this archetype is the martyr's need to be rewarded for her sacrifices with either gratitude or dependency. If others do not appreciate their devotion, some martyrs can be resentful or hurt. Neither do martyrs always understand that their giving may be crippling to others who may need to experience life's trials for themselves in order to attain their autonomy.

The martyr may also use giving as an evasion of personal growth in other areas (e.g., "I'd love to take this professional development workshop but my disabled wife needs me at home and I can't possibly impose on someone to sit with her for a few days while I'm gone").

The challenge in the lives of martyrs may be to find alternate ways than giving to find personal fulfillment. Sometimes it is as hard for martyrs *not to give* as it is for a selfish person to give!

For the lifewriter, the challenge is to differentiate between the positive and negative aspects of this archetype. The writer needs to explore how successful his subject was in combining the need to give with the need to pursue other areas of self-growth and with others' needs to be autonomous.

B) *People who do not develop or maintain personal ties can be said to be pursuing the orphan archetype.* Artists are an example of the positive side of the orphan archetype. Because they feel detached from roots, family, etc, "orphan" artists are free to tell the truth as they see it, to risk much in the pursuit of their art. On the negative side, the orphan is a person who throws everything out too easily and who starts again from scratch time after time. While artists make use of their rootlessness to create, non-artists may be oppressed by their own tendency to destroy what they have accomplished.

Orphans often feel besieged by life, alone against the superior forces of the universe. In retaliation, they may react to life with cynicism and bitterness. Orphans also love to tell you they are self-made-- and will neglect to tell you of any help they received. Orphans have a tendency to remake the facts to support their self-made world view.

When writing about an orphan, the lifewriter needs to appreciate the struggle the orphan has waged, but the

The person who says she wants to write her lifestories but always allows herself to be interrupted by her family's demands is an example of the martyr who uses her giving to avoid doing important personal work.

The person who is always telling you how he did everything for himself in his life, how no one ever gave him anything, is an example of the orphan.

writer must also assess whether this orphan was blinded to the many favors life offered and to the support that was available. The lifewriter needs to explore what orphans used for roots and community in life, how they overcame their pervasive sense of alone-ness and abandonment. Since orphans tend to remake the facts to support their self-made images, writers should be especially careful to verify information orphans give them with other sources.

C) *A third and last example taken from the many possible is the prince-left-at-the-pauper's-door.* These people are imbued with a sense of their innate worth. They may happen to be poor at the moment but they are really "princes" (or "princesses") and have a right to special ("royal") status in life. Princes-left-at-the-pauper's-door aspire to be more and to have more than might seem reasonable to others, and they often have the strength and the courage to match their will to achieve. An example is the immigrant who arrives in a new country penniless and sees no reason why he should not rise "from rags to riches" in this foreign society. Another example is a poor child who aspires to a fine education in the midst of inferior schools and intellectual wastelands.

People who come out of modest backgrounds and achieve highly are often rejected by their siblings and former friends who have not achieved as much.

Of course, there is a negative side to the prince-left-at-the-pauper's-door archetype too. These people may look disdainfully on the other "paupers" among whom they live ("I'm too good for these peons!") and so cut themselves off from participating in the community available to them. The prince-left-at-the-pauper's-door may be as lonely as the orphan. Inevitably, too, the high achiever, whether disdainful of others or not, will attract the resentment of many who have been, or are being, left behind.

The lifewriter must look carefully at these princes-left-at-the-pauper's-door to distinguish which parts of their struggles were necessary and inevitable for attaining their goals and which parts were injurious to them (forsaking relationships, for instance).

The Cinderella is a princess-left-at-the-pauper's-door. She waits for a Prince Charming to save her from the unpleasant drudgeries and responsibilities of her life.

✐ **Writing from the perspective of personal myths can explain a lot about the stories you are recording.** In addition, consciously living the archetypes in your own life and turning them into positive forces is a rewarding path for self-growth.

✐ **Although archetypes can be compared to animal**

instincts, they are not as fixed. They are inclinations which we are both born with *and* molded to. They are strengthened by many factors, one among them being family ranking.

Older children in a family, for instance, tend to be rewarded for being martyrs. Parents need their help to manage younger children. Encouraging an oldest child to be a wanderer or a dreamer would get in the way of accomplishing the routine tasks that need to be done to maintain a large family. (The older child whose dominant archetype is that of the wanderer or dreamer may then compromise and assume the role of victim which accomplishes the work for the parents but also gets its revenge by casting guilt on them.)

A youngest child is sometimes the product of older parents who are financially more at ease than when the first child was young. The parents may want to have more fun with parenting than was available to them with the older children. They therefore encourage the "baby" to take on the archetype of a magician, a clown-- a person less focused on practicalities who is both more fun to be with and less likely to grow away from them too fast.

✐ **Our archetypes are not the only elements which create our personal myths.** Other people's responses to us and the culture in which we live play significant roles.

✐ **Lifewriting,** in as much as it enables us to become aware of the various elements that have created our personal myths, **empowers us to choose the stories we will live out in our lives.** As you write about yourself or about other people, be attentive to your active personal myths and interpret your stories in light of them. And know, too, that some of your lifestories are not yet finished. Insights you gain from the past can be put to good use in your present and your future.

"People must not dissolve into a whirl of warring possibilities and tendencies imposed upon them by the unconscious, but must become the unity that embraces all possibilities and tendencies."
- C.G. Jung
psychoanalyst

"Because I was the oldest child, my parents needed me to protect the younger ones. When I married, I continued to play this role with my wife. We found it a comfortable role."
- Workshop writer

Exercise

✔ Finish the following sentence: There was once a (man-- or boy) (woman-- or girl) who...

Make up a story, even if it seems fantastical, that comes readily to your mind about this character. Give free rein to your imagination. Write for as long as you want. *Do not read the rest of this exercise until you have done this writing.*

✔ Here is an example of how you might have started your story. "There was once a man who did his best in his life. He wasn't the most intelligent or the richest or the most skilled man there was, but he undertook each challenge with as much skill and intelligence as he could muster, etc."

✔ Another example: "There was once a girl who curled up in her mommy's lap. She was very comfortable there and she didn't want to have to get up. One day, her mommy's lap seemed smaller and, every day afterwards, it got smaller and smaller, etc."

✔ Now reread your story. In the place of boy or woman (or other word you wrote in), insert your own name. What does this story now say about *you?* (Yes, it really is about some part of you!) In what sense does the story you have just written reveal a myth in your life? How does acknowledging this myth help you to understand what you have lived and how you really feel about it? How can it help you give more depth to your stories? more awareness to your life?

F. Don't preach to me!

The negative underside of theme is *preachiness.* You preach when you insist on your reader endorsing your theme, message, or point of view.

✐ **Here's a way to distinguish between preachiness and the right use of theme.** Read your text out loud to yourself. If you have been preachy, *your grand, all-inclusive phrases will jump out at you.* Sometimes, in *Turning Memories Into Memoirs* workshops, people begin to laugh as they read aloud such phrases as:

> *This section conveys how the misuse of theme can backfire in lifewriting.*

"I'd like to see how many kids today would..."
"In those days, we weren't afraid to..."
"If you're going to do it right, you have to..."
"The evil we see today is due to..."

"Teenagers today don't realize how important little things in life are" is the beginning of a sermon. It is not the start of an insight.

On the other hand, "It was all I had for Christmas and it didn't matter to me then. We were all together and for that I was grateful" is not at all preachy. It states your reaction which the reader is free to accept or reject.

Now let's alter this last example: "It was all I had for Christmas. Kids today wouldn't have been satisfied, but it didn't matter to me then." That little phrase *kids today wouldn't have been satisfied*, as innocuous or true as it may seem, is preachy. *As a grand, all-inclusive statement, it is likely to cost you your reader's attention.* You lose credibility when you promote your *particular* experience as a *universal* truth.

In writing your story, you are sharing your experience and perhaps that of your generation, or ethnic group, or religious/philosophical community. Tell your story. Period. Don't thrust it on the reader as an example of the life-well-lived or of your superiority.

G. The glazed-over-eyes test

1) Sixteen year-olds have a built in preachiness detector. Remember one of your children or grandchildren at sixteen (or for that matter: you!) at a time he might have had a problem or unhappy situation.

Suppose an adult had said the following to this young person, "This is what you need to do..."

Would the teenager's eyes have glazed over? Would he have gotten angry, have changed the subject and grown distant?

Or would he have thanked the adult profusely for setting him straight!

When you were preached at when you were sixteen, did you go out and alter your life to accommodate the advice? Fat chance!

Now imagine a slightly different development to the exchange. Instead of saying "This is what you need to do...", the adult might have said, "Once, I had a similar situation and this is what I did."

Doesn't the prospect of a child or a grandchild asking, "What do you think about what you did? Is there anything you would have done differently?" seem much more likely now than when the adult got preachy?

Remember: a way to avoid preachiness is to focus on the individual. The next time you question whether or not your writing is preachy, try applying this litmus test: read your stories to a sixteen year old!

2) **Be subtle rather than heavy-handed.** Literature (as is true for any art form) works best on a subconscious level. Art can change lives. Your story is more likely to uplift and inform if its theme is subtly presented. In fact, the reader will resist your preachiness and stop reading (just as the sixteen year old stops listening) if you use too-heavy a hand.

The guidance your stories can provide is a major function of the tale well told. Stories rehearse us for living the future; they reassure us that we are not alone in our struggles; and they show us that we all share common problems. Don't let your preachiness get in the way of your story.

Trudy Laliberté in her Cadet Nurse Corps uniform, 1944

Lifestories from the Workshops:

Little Did I Know *by Trudy Laliberté*

Little did I know that America's involvement in World War II would steer me towards the selection of a fulfilling and financially-rewarding career.

In September of 1939, I entered Lewiston High School without an immediate or long range career goal. I enrolled in the commercial course, believing that office work would be my future. My parents' lives had been full of uphill struggles due to illness and financial difficulties. Their lives had revolved around work and family, making of these a strong ethic. This made a deep and lasting impression on me. I felt strongly that my life must somehow be different, but I wasn't sure how. When I was a teenager, as a means of survival, I continued their pattern of work.

I worked my way through high school doing odd jobs. They were monotonous, demeaning and unchallenging. Between 1939 and 1943 therefore, I spent holidays and weekends hulling strawberries at a commercial packing company, picking string beans at a farm, affixing labels to bottles at the Gin Distribution Company. I hand-packed donuts at Lepage's Bakery, sold candy at J.J. Newbury's and cosmetics at F.W. Woolworth's. I babysat for a local family, and worked as a spinner-cleaner at the Hill Mill. I was a tack puller at the Clark Shoe Shop, a rod examiner at North American Philips Electronics. Putting up with the sights, the sounds, and the smells of these jobs was the only challenge.

> *The writer of this story discovered a dominant theme that had characterized her life since girlhood. She shows insight not only into her own behavior but also into that of her parents and her brother.*

There were positive effects to all of this, however: if I could survive these four years of menial work, I could survive anything and I knew it. And my resolve to prepare myself for a lifetime of challenging work that provided both variety and adequate compensation was strengthened. I vowed to seek a future free of my parents' struggles, a future that would be personally and financially rewarding. I wanted also to be able to provide my parents with a life of greater ease and comfort.

In early 1940, I still had no clue as to a career direction or a course of action to accomplish these goals. But an unexpected appendectomy that summer turned my life around.

I spent three weeks in the hospital and observed the nurses at work. Their skill, compassion and positive attitudes inspired me to join their ranks.

I mulled the idea over: how could I ever finance three additional years of study after high school? It didn't seem possible, so I continued with the commercial courses, and nursing became a dormant goal. I believed I had no alternative to office work-- until World War II came to my rescue!

Following Pearl Harbor and the declaration of war, my idea of becoming a nurse resurfaced. I could follow my brother's patriotic example and be of service to my country if only I could find the financial resources to put myself through nursing school.

In 1942, an Act of Congress was passed creating the U.S. Cadet Nurse Corps. The program's purpose was to prepare additional military nurses for service. As soon as I heard about it, I went to a local hospital for more information. It seemed possible that I would qualify.

In 1942, I returned to high school for my junior year and switched from the commercial course to a special course created for those of us who were preparing for the Cadet Nurse program. I dropped typing, bookkeeping and stenography and took up instead Latin, biology, chemistry, algebra and college English.

A retiree, Trudy Laliberté earned a Nursing B.S.(Boston College) and an M.S. in Nursing Administration (the Catholic University of America). She now enjoys driving along the scenic backroads of rural Maine and doing a variety of crafts, as well as cooking and helping others.

In September 1943, at the beginning of my senior year, I was accepted into the first class of the U.S. Cadet Nurse Program and entered St. Mary's School of Nursing. The government paid all my educational expenses and provided a monthly stipend of $10 the first year, $20 the second, and $30 the third year. After graduation, the cadets were obligated to serve a minimum of two years in one of the branches of the military service.

The academic and clinical programs were accelerated to ready the cadets for mobilization within eighteen months if necessary. We spent the first three months on an intense schedule: six days a week, we began our clinical work at 7 AM. At 9 AM, we had four hours of classes, then back to the nursing units until 7 PM. We were expected to absorb and retain information and skills rapidly during these twelve hour days.

I was proud to wear the Cadet Nurse uniform: slate gray woolen suits with bright red epaulets, and modified French berets for the winter, and pin-striped light gray and white uniforms for the summer.

The war ended in 1945. I was to graduate from the program the following June. Though I was happy that the war was over and that men and women would be coming home and be able to continue with their lives, I was disappointed that I would not be fulfilling my military obligations.

I entertained the notion of joining the Army Nurse Corps nonetheless, though the idea was distressing to my mother. She had worried and prayed long enough over my brother's well-being, she insisted. She wouldn't, couldn't, go through that again. At last I gave it up.

Years later, I discovered the reason for my mother's persistent objections to my joining the army. My brother had written many letters to her advising her at all costs to keep me from joining any military branch. I felt quite let down by this brother whom I had supported and prayed for during his life-threatening service in the South Pacific.

I had accomplished my goals: to be a nurse and to be able to make my parents' lives more comfortable. The public however, was the main beneficiary from my 36-year professional career, rather than the military forces. The public has been well-served and my government-funded education has been fully repaid.

Chapter 7   "I Need to Know..."

A.   Writers need to be readers, too!

B.   Take time out from writing.

C.   Let's get personal.

D.   Therapy

E.   Journal keeping

F.   Men and lifewriting

G.   Be a "real" writer.

H.   Vive la différence: using foreign words

I.   Buying a word processor

J.   Tape recording your stories

Lifestories from the Workshops:
Memorial Day by Doris Stevens

Any questions, please...

Writing your lifestory is highly personal. *Turning Memories Into Memoirs* offers guidelines to maximize that experience but it shies away from presenting fixed procedures because what will seem immediately compelling for one lifewriter may not interest another for a long time. The questions answered in this chapter sometimes get asked early in one workshop while in another they might not come up at all until I bring them up for consideration. In this chapter, as in the rest of this book, read first the material that seems most useful to you.

> *This chapter answers some questions that come up during lifewriting workshops.*

A. Writers need to be readers, too.

Q. Will reading make me a better lifewriter?

A. Absolutely! Imitation can teach you a lot about effective writing techniques as you grow to develop your own style. Reading good stories will help you to write good stories.

In general, read widely and voluminously. In particular, read memoirs, autobiographies, and biographies. (See Appendix B for a reading list.) Read not only in books but in magazines. Photocopy magazine stories you've enjoyed so that you can reread them later.

Read as a writer-- i.e., study how others have handled their stories. What can you repeat-- or use as inspiration?

> *It makes as much sense for a writer not to read as for a composer not to go to concerts or for an athlete not to attend sporting events or for a gardener not to look at other people's gardens.*

How do the writers introduce their *characters* and their *action* (look at those opening paragraphs)? How do they develop the various *conflicts* that make up the action of their stories? Has the technique of *suspense* been used? Have the writers started *close enough to the final crisis or climax*? What are the *turning points* of their stories and how are the conflicts resolved? Have they used *specific and striking details* in describing characters, actions, and settings? Is *point of view* used effectively? Is the *tone* in each story appropriate for its theme? Is the theme presented without *preachiness*? How are *unpleasant truths* handled? How have the authors *ended their stories* (scrutinize the last paragraphs)? How do these writers handle their *transitions* from one segment (and one story) of their lives to another?

Reading beyond technical matters, see how others have dealt with stories whose topics or themes are similar to yours. What effective elements do these stories contain that you have not included in your own story? What fresh perspectives does this create for you?

Certainly, at the very least, reading this material will jog your memory and give you an expanded sense of possibilities. Don't forget: the more you know, the more detailed the background of your writing will be and the fuller your stories will become.

B. Take time out from writing.

"Why is it I get my best ideas in the morning while shaving?"
- A. Einstein
scientist

Q. How will I know the difference between avoiding writing and taking time out to let an idea mature?

A. Writing is hard work, and there will be many times when it will seem too difficult to do. You will sit at your desk to write and not much will come. Your instinct will be to get up to do something else-- anything as long as it is not writing. You will think of the pencils that need to be sharpened, of the closet that needs to be sorted out, etc.

To distinguish between avoiding writing and letting an idea ripen, think for a moment about doing physical exercise. You may not always enjoy exercising, but I bet you know the difference between not exercising because you are not enjoying it and not exercising because of another reason that has nothing to do with avoidance: for example, you are sick or your schedule is too full. After you avoid exercise, you are likely to feel guilty; after putting it off for other reasons, what you feel is disappointment and impatience to return to your routine.

The effects of writing and not writing are similar to those of exercising and not exercising. When you avoid writing, you feel that you are not meeting your goals. You may even feel guilty. If this is the case, remind yourself of your writing objectives, reread your mission statement, and rededicate yourself to the task and its rewards.

There will be other times, however, when your writing is not coming easily and, rather than force yourself to continue, you will feel you must put your pen down and go out for a walk. You may feel a bit jumbled at first, but, as you clean house, make the beds, or have a cup of tea while listening to music, you are aware that you are still grappling with your story-- and not at all avoiding it. Suddenly an idea comes up out of "nowhere" and, *voilà*, you understand your story. Or, perhaps the breakthrough presents itself later that day or the next day over a stack of dishes, or in the quiet of the forest, or as you look out the window on a snow storm.

If you write many stories, at least some of them will require this kind of time out. Don't be afraid to let it happen. Do not force your writing; give yourself some time to step back to reflect on your experience.

"Forcing the emotions brings errors; letting them come naturally is the way to make them clear."
- Lu Chi
philosopher

"As for my next book, I am going to hold myself back from writing it till I have it impending in me: grown heavy in my mind like a ripe pear; pendant, gravid, asking to be cut or it will fall."
- Virginia Woolf
novelist

C. Let's get personal.

Q. Isn't it self-important to record my inner life?
A. Not at all! Our lives are composed not only of facts and dates but also of dreams and expectations and hopes. You are not alone to have had an inner life-- you will more likely attract praise rather than scorn for sharing it.

If there is any place where you can say, "This is who I really was and am", where you can help others understand the hero's journey you have undertaken, it is in your lifestories. Here, you can document the inner changes and the turmoils, the psychological victories or defeats that have made you the person you are today.

There are several benefits that you will derive from doing this.

"The soul becomes dyed with the color of its thoughts."
- Marcus Aurelius
Roman emperor

✐ **You will likely grow to esteem the inner journey you have taken in your life and to appreciate the uniqueness of your response to life.** If you have not always lived your life wisely, what better time than now for you to come to terms with that, too. You can now begin to adapt the way in which you go about being yourself. You will see new ways that will serve not only your survival but also your development better if you allow yourself the insights lifewriting offers.

✐ **Your readers will most certainly be comforted.** By not holding back, you will provide others with the reassurance and guidance each of them desperately needs, and even craves, as they make their ways through their own lives.

✐ **Your family history, too, has a story of inner events that needs and deserves to be recorded.** Understanding family history-- in its entirety-- can set you and your descendants free from unhealthy inheritances. Conversely, those who ignore their family histories are perhaps destined to repeat them. Don't let your family down by settling for a mere chronology of dates or catalogue of facts. There is so much more that needs to be written!

Remember: you do not need to share every scrap of writing you produce. It is all right for you to write something that you have no intention of ever sharing with anyone! *Once you have benefited from the insights a piece of writing provides, it is all right for you to throw it away or to store it where only you will ever see it.*

Writing the inner version of your lifestory (even if you decide not to share it with anyone else) will be a valuable affirmation-- to you-- of your life's journey. This journey of exploration is as old as the human race itself. Recording it is not at all vulgar or self-important. Rather, it provides guidance and reassurance to those who come after you.

Exercise

✔ Write your obituary as if you were a reporter. Tell the world about this person who was yourself. What animated the life of this person? What are the qualities of mind and spirit (vs. what you *did*) that you should be remembered for?

✔ Look at your lifestories. Have you incorporated in them the qualities that you wrote about in your obituary?

D. Therapy

Q. I still don't understand: why does lifewriting feel so much like therapy sometimes?

A. We all have *façades*, images of ourselves we are willing to make public. When you meet someone at a party or for the first time, it is the public self you are meeting. Much later, if you become friends, you may have access to his private self.

Unfortunately, living with a *façade* can sometimes make us strangers even to ourselves. When people write their lifestories, they often give themselves permission to go beyond the public *façade* of the stories they and their families have told about themselves.

Acknowledging one's true self is a healing experience. The more truthful you are as you write and the more deeply you penetrate your experience, the more integrating and thus the more healing the practice of lifewriting becomes.

Our lives fall out of balance as we live others' versions of who we were, are, or should be. Writing our lifestories helps us to accept *our* versions and to eliminate others' so that, ultimately, we can become ourselves.

Psychological therapy, at its best, integrates how we view our lives with how we live them. It also provides us with the strength to stop living behind *façades* and other people's versions of us. That's why lifewriting and therapy resemble each other a lot.

"Writing is a form of therapy; how do all those who do not write, compose, or paint manage to escape the madness, the melancholia, the panic and fear which is inherent in the human condition?"
- Graham Greene
novelist

Is TMIM more an awareness-raising than a writing workshop? It's both-- the two dancing gracefully together.

E. Journal keeping

Writer's block may be another way of saying that you are not letting your unconscious impulses surface. Linger more with your writing and trust your intuition.

"If there is a secret to writing, I haven't found it yet. All I know is sit down, clear your mind, and hang in there."
- Mary McGrory
columnist

Q. What tool or technique can you suggest to overcome writer's block-- and lack of fluency?

A. When keeping a regular (even daily) journal, some people feel a release of energy that they do not feel in other writing forms. Journal keeping can be an important developmental experience for you both as a person and as a writer. Because the journal is private by definition, you can write in it without any fear of audience. No one will ever see it. *Not ever*-- unless you want them to!

1) **Think of the journal as a laboratory.** Scientists use a laboratory to conduct experiments. They check what results from adding this to that, from changing relationships and quantities and sequences. Sometimes when the results are interesting and prove worth pursuing, they continue conducting experiments in similar areas, pairing these findings with those from other experiments.

The journal can be a sort of writing laboratory for you. What happens when you record your dreams? What if you make lists? What if you do free associations of ideas? What if you recreate the past as you wish it had been? (Give yourself a commanding role! Have everything turn out "the way it was supposed to"!)

You can also experiment with various styles and techniques to record your feelings and perceptions. What if you write only in long sentences? or only in short ones? Never use the word "I"? Or use stream of consciousness (thoughts written without any editing)?

Perhaps your writing block is due to being cramped by the limits you have imposed on yourself. Try using your journal as a place to break free.

2) **The journal will help you be fluent in your writing even if you do not experiment.** As in anything, the more you do, the better you are likely to become. Swim every day and, after a month, you'll find yourself having become much better at it-- and a whole lot better after six months. Writing in your journal regularly, you will get a lot of practice time. Your writing will grow to be a more familiar experience, and you will be more fluent with it.

3) **Writing in your journal before you start your**

lifewriting sessions can be a great warm-up. Athletes do not start their sports immediately without warming up. Why shouldn't a writer warm up, too? Limber up your writing muscles with a page or two of journal writing.

4) **Journal writing will provide you with perceptions that you can make use of when writing your lifestories.** If you assure yourseslf of the journal's absolute inviolability, the inner censor who insists "You can't write that!" will recede. You will feel free to write your feelings and thoughts. Later, many of your entries or parts of them can be transcribed into your lifestories as you give yourself permission to try different versions of the official story line. In the privacy of the journal, you will grow comfortable with your new "heretical" versions.

Have you made a journal list of people from your past? You can include that list in your lifestories. Why not?

Have you made a "word portrait" of the horse you loved dearly as an adolescent? Transcribe it from your journal into one of your stories.

In your journal, as a free association, you've written ten words that describe your mother. You can include the words, as is, in your lifestory. You can also use each of the words as a jumping off point to create scenes.

Whatever you do in your journal where there are few rules (*honesty* being one of the few), you can replicate it in your lifestories (where there are some requirements). You will always do so to your great benefit.

To write well-- honestly, deeply, connectedly-- about someone, you need to write out of some spot of affection or respect. Otherwise you will record "stick" figures that do not pull anyone into your text.

F. Men and lifewriting

Q. Why do fewer men than women do lifewriting?

A. I don't know why it is that fewer men write their lifestories. Perhaps the reason is as simple as that men in our culture do not have permission from women and from other men to express their feelings. Perhaps men in our culture have been made to feel that introspection is not in keeping with being masculine (whatever that may be). Perhaps they have been made to accept that passing on a family's culture is a woman's responsibility.

In the many *Turning Memories Into Memoirs* workshops I have presented, there have always been fewer men than women. Men are also more likely to drop out. Why this should be so is all the more difficult to understand since many artists and philosophers are men and as such they explore both the feeling life and the depths of the psyche. This is the very domain in which lifewriting excels.

When I have assigned exercises, I have seen men turn to their wives and ask, "Now why was it I did that?" One man even asked his wife, "What were the important events in my life?"

Since at least the advent of the Industrial Revolution, society has had a vested interest in keeping men far from their feelings. However else could a man accept to spend his life at a job that as often as not has no meaning for him! Our society would collapse if men refused to do the work they are urged from boyhood to do-- urged by both their fathers and their mothers.

Although some men do break the stereotypes-- often at the great price to themselves of being seen as less "masculine"-- to become artists and philosophers, many more are not willing to work with what is perceived as a "feminine" medium.

Undertaking the challenges of lifewriting can go against the indoctrination of a lifetime. Contacting one's feelings is a powerful experience-- and therefore frightening in many ways! Yet ultimately, it is the healthiest task a person of either gender can undertake.

Liberate a man in your life-- your mate, your father, your son-- so that he can connect with his feelings. Buy him a copy of *Turning Memories Into Memoirs*, and support his lifewriting in every way you can.

G. Be a "real" writer.

Q. *Will lifewriting make me into a 'real' writer?*
A. Perhaps you have approached lifewriting with a hidden agenda. Have you wanted to be a "writer"-- even a "Writer"-- for a long time but aren't sure about how to do it? Perhaps you've been a reader all your life and feel you

might have a book or two in you. Perhaps a novel. Or are magazines and newspapers where you want to see your work in print?

Have you come to lifewriting with the hope that it will somehow transform you into a "writer" (or was that "Writer")?

In workshops, a hopeful participant will ask me, "Do you think I'm good enough to be a 'real' writer?"

It's impossible to answer this question directly. In an often quoted letter, Rainer Maria Rilke answered a young writer who had written to him to ask this very question. Rilke wrote, "You must ask how much you *need* to be a writer."

Writing is not easy. Most writers don't write for money: there generally isn't much to be had anyway. They don't write for fame either because that generally evades most writers. Writers write because the process is important to them.

Writing if you are going to do it regularly, every day even, must be impelled by an inner force. It is one experience to write as you feel moved to do so-- perhaps early in the morning over a hot drink or on a rainy afternoon when you can't do anything else-- or to write short pieces that entertain you or your friends. It is another experience altogether to undertake a long project, a book of several hundred pages-- especially when the book requires tight writing, some sustained imagery and tone. Writing then becomes more like a job. It is a task that calls for discipline and commitment.

Unlike many other "jobs", writing is speculative. When you go to work and have a bad day, you still get paid. When you have a bad day at writing, you have a wastebasket full of paper and no pay. So if you are going to keep writing, there has to be something else driving you.

Most people who come to lifewriting do not want to be "real" writers, of course. If you are one of these or if being a "Writer" seems either too remote or too emotionally taxing for you, perhaps you can enjoy being a "writer"! Many people have seen portions of their lifestories printed in magazines and newspapers. They have experienced their work reaching out to others-- and isn't the hometown crowd the most satisfying one to reach?

"Desire is where perseverance comes from, where a certain necessary stubbornness comes from, and finally, it should be what makes people try to become better in the absolute sense."
- Madison Smartt Bell
writer

"Ask yourself in the stillest hour of the night: must I write?"
- R.M. Rilke
poet

"Work inspires inspiration. Keep working. If you succeed, keep working. If you fail, keep working. If you're interested, keep working. If you're bored, keep working."
- Michael Crichton
novelist

"This lifewriting is hard work!"
- Workshop writer

Do you remember fondly an amusement park that is no longer standing? Write about your fun and adventures there and see your story published in the local newspapers on an anniversary date.

Were you active in an organization? Perhaps its newspaper or magazine could use your reminiscences?

Did you have an important decision to make at your job or did you work for someone who did? What magazine or newspaper would be pleased to publish this story?

Don't let "success" at writing be defined by someone else! Determine for yourself what your criteria for success will be.

If you keep in mind that newspapers and magazines are always looking for seasonal and historical stories: e.g., holiday customs, gardening practices of yesteryear, etc., you will find yourself a "real" writer one day even if you aren't published in New York.

H. Vive la différence: using foreign words

Q. My grandchildren don't speak our language anymore. Should I eliminate all non-English words and phrases from my text?

Why should society be a melting pot? Think of it as a tossed salad filled with different tastes and textures, each waiting to be enjoyed. A bowl of plain iceberg lettuce?! Not for me, thanks!

A. My preference is to use foreign words in lifestories because it recreates a world that was once yours. That's what you are doing with your writing: celebrating a world that no longer exists. Leonore Burke's story (page 36) would be impoverished had she eliminated *Babcia* in favor of *grandmother*, *keilbasa* for *sausage stuffing*. These and many other "foreign" (to us but not to her) words in her text give us the flavor of the home and community she grew up in.

One way to make sure that these words are understood is to do any one of the following:

✐ include a translation in parenthesis immediately after you have used the word-- e.g. *placek* (a sweet Polish bread).

✐ paraphrase the word or phrase right away-- e.g. "*Arrête!*" she said. "Stop!"

✐ provide a translation in a footnote at the end of your

book or at the bottom of the page.

Remember: whenever you use a non-English word, you need to italicize it.

I. Buying a computer

Q. Should I get a word processing computer?

A. If you intend to write more than a handful of stories-- certainly if you intend to write more than fifty pages, I urge you to buy a computer word processor. The difference between typewriting and word processing is like the difference between a washboard and an automatic washer.

Writing your stories will require significant emotional and artistic commitment. Why add to it the drudgery of typing page after page over and over again?

Word processing makes every mechanical step of getting your story recorded so much easier. For instance, when you are typing, adding a sentence at the beginning of your manuscript entails typing the whole story over again or eliminating another sentence with the same number of words so that your next page starts at the same place as before the insertion. This takes a lot of time-- as often as not, you may decide to leave out the addition rather than retype.

"You mean I won't have to sit down every night and force myself to type three pages until I catch up with my stories?"
        - Workshop writer

With a word processor, you merely type the sentence in and print a new copy. This will take only a few minutes. A word processor also eliminates the need for correction tapes and their clumsy and time-consuming erasures.

The advantages go on and on. I can't recommend highly enough that you get yourself a word processor.

Don't depend on a computer store for guidance however. The people there are in the business of selling you an item they have in stock rather than of providing you with real information that may send you to their competitor. Instead, find a relative or friend who can advise you. Computer literacy is now so widespread that it is highly unlikely that you don't know someone who can advise you. Ask around for a used system. There are many out there that you can get relatively cheaply to meet your needs. You might also look into typewriters with word processing units.

The first month you use a word processor is likely to be awkward. Don't give up. Once you get used to word processing, its advantages are so incredible that you will wonder why you waited so long to get a system.

"So what if I've never been handy with machines! I'm tired of typing."
- Workshop writer

J. Tape recording your stories

Q. Is tape recording a story okay? I don't like writing.
A. Preserving a story in any form is always better than letting it be lost. Audio-taping a story can be a marvelous way to record people's voices and all that reveals about their lives. (You might also think of video-taping.)

Taping can be a creative option, but it is not necessarily easier than writing. If that's what you are really implying (that taping is going to be easier than writing), you are in for a surprise.

"She had an old-time New Foundland accent. I've got it down on tape."
- Workshop writer

You can, of course, record stories "off the cuff", but these will have the same rough quality as first drafts of a written story.

✐ **You will need to prepare your recording with the same lifelists that a writer makes.** Elements in your lifelist will have to be grouped together. You will have to decide whether you want to link your stories chronologically, thematically, biographically or by the era.

✐ **You will need to grapple with the questions of** *theme* as you try to make meaning out of your life's experience.

✐ **You will have to deal with** *truth.* What is it and how much of it should you tell?

✐ **You will need to conduct interviews and do research to make sure your facts are correct.** You will have to make use of memory jogs.

✐ **You will face pain and experience the therapeutic effects of telling your story.**

✐ **You will have to listen to your story and have others listen to it to help you to edit it.** You will have to retell it in the same way that a writer has to re-write.

My own preference is both written stories and interview recordings of the people you are writing about. Tapes need tape players; books can be opened anytime, anyplace. Books are bigger and so less likely to be misplaced. And, you can't erase a book in the same way you can a tape.

Lifestories from the Workshops:

Memorial Day *by Doris B. Stevens*

Doris Bagley Stevens worked in bookstores as an adult. She has one daughter and one granddaughter.

In the 1920s, in Cape Elizabeth, Maine, we celebrated Memorial Day on May 30th. We sometimes called it Decoration Day. It was a day to honor those who gave their lives for their country. At that time, there were men and women still living who had served in the Civil War and in World War I. Many of the women were the much-loved Red Cross nurses. The lovely old war song, "The Rose of No-man's Land" was a tribute to them.

By mid-morning, most homes and public buildings displayed the American flag. Lilacs blooming in many yards filled the air with their sweet fragrance.

The sound of martial music was heard as a small band of musicians gathered by the little white country church. A green-lawned cemetery surrounded three sides of the church. We school children, each carrying a small flag, were lined up by a teacher from one of the schools. Some of us girls carried sprays of white or purple lilacs to place on the graves of the soldiers and sailors.

To one side stood four well-known local folk who took on a special aura for this occasion. Together, they made up a vocal quartet. On any other day they were farmers and farm wives we might have chatted with freely, but today, at this quiet place, they were strangers whose songs brought tears to our eyes.

One of our schoolmates, always a boy, chosen to recite the Gettysburg Address, stood near the singers. Three of my brothers had been chosen for this honor. Mama had coached them well.

Family and friends stood near the white rail fence enclosing the tree-shaded graveyard. Some stood at the graves of their own dear ones, a hushed group.

The band began and an honor guard led us into the yard. At each veteran's burial place a small flag was set, a bouquet of lilacs was gently laid. Then a smart salute was given as every patriot was recognized. The band ceased. Softly the harmony of the quartet hung over us as the old, old songs-- "Tenting Tonight", "The Vacant Chair", "The Battle Cry of Freedom"-- were sung.

These were sad and sweet moments.

The music ended and the reciter stepped out before the honor guard. Once again a young boy's voice rang out with Lincoln's famous words. He could only imagine what war might be, though in the case of two of my brothers, they discovered for themselves in World War II-- the war that would never happen again!

The haunting notes of "Taps" playing in the distance ended our Memorial Day tribute. The band and honor guard moved on to other cemeteries where the ceremony would be repeated.

We children now seemed to need a parent's hand to hold as we quietly left the churchyard for safe and familiar home. For a little while, we had experienced a different world, a shared reverence. As I walked along, clinging to Mama as she carried my baby sister, I could hear the gentle song,

> We shall meet, but we shall miss him.
> There will be one vacant chair.
> We shall linger to caress him
> While we breathe our evening prayer.*

---

* *from the Civil War song, "The Vacant Chair" by George E. Root.*

Chapter 8   *"This is a Little Thing, but ... "*

A.   Use a note pad.
B.   What about the writing order?
C.   The active vs. the passive voice
D.   The third person
E.   Is good grammar needed?
F.   Say it once. Period.
G.   What's verisimilitude?
H.   Avoid clichés and stereotypes.
I.   Be complete and concise.
J.   Use precise language.
K.   The 10% rule: be more concise!

Lifestories from the Workshops:
Tillie *by Bill Fagan*

Make it easier for yourself...

"Where's the best place to jot down a memory that pops up suddenly?" someone might ask in a workshop.

Another might say, "I wrote a story about myself but I used the third person. Is that all right?"

"How about good grammar? Is that always necessary?"

This chapter provides answers to these questions and to others like them.

> This chapter will offer workable answers to questions that writers often ask in workshops about some day-to-day aspects of lifewriting.

A. Use a note pad.

Q. How do I keep from losing ideas that come to me "out of the blue"?

A. After they commit themselves to writing, lifewriters report that scenes, conversations, and images from the past come quickly and unexpectedly. The same writers who feared they would not have enough memories to write about come to feel they have too many to handle!

If memories and ideas come to you quickly and unexpectedly-- at the grocery store, waiting in your car for a light to change, watching TV at your sister's, try keeping a pocket-size notebook handy to record them. Your notes can be mere jottings ("Aunt Elsie wore a fur coat made of skins caught by Uncle Fred") or they can be whole stories that pour out on the spur of the moment.

At your writing desk, later, you can incorporate your jottings into a story or use the details in a longer piece. You can also file the material under an appropriate head-

> "Make notes-- I've lost more material than I've ever written. Contrary to popular opinion, it's not still up there in one's brain. It's in outer space and it ain't coming back."
> - Judith Guest
> *novelist*

Use a tape player to record a story you suddenly recall as you are driving.

ing to retrieve it later.

✐ *It is a good idea, too, to keep a notebook next to your bed to record your dreams,* those wonderful out-pourings of the unconscious. If you pay regular attention to your dreams, they will provide clues to understanding your past. They will even reveal something meaningful about those events and relationships which may not have made sense to you before.

✐ *A note pad will almost surely preserve you from the anxiety* that can come from the fear of losing good scenes, conversations, and images when you do not take notes. With ideas jotted down on your pad, instead of feeling anxious, you will be eager to get back to your writing desk and continue with your writing!

B. What about writing order?

"The last thing that we find in making a book is to know what we must put first."
- Blaise Pascal
philosopher

Q. Is there a correct sequence to writing my stories?
A. No. People sometimes think that they should write according to the order on their lifelist of important people and events. They feel compelled to begin from the first item on the list and proceed systematically to the last (often somewhere near the present).

If it feels good to proceed in a 1-2-3 order (not to begin the second story until you have completed the first), go ahead. But if it doesn't feel good to do that, you don't have to write according to an order. There's another way.

✐ **Start wherever you feel like starting**-- in the middle or at the end, anywhere. The third piece you write may ultimately be the first piece in your story sequence, while what you had written first may fit toward the end.

✐ **Try this too: don't feel compelled to write entire stories at once.** It's not only acceptable but potentially more creative to write fragments (scenes, conversations, images) on separate sheets. *Write as inspiration moves you;* that is, at random, in snippets. A benefit to proceeding this way is that your stories get composed bit by bit-- which, for many lifewriters, is easier than writing many pages at one sitting!

Once you have written a number of fragments or completed stories, arrange them in an order appropriate to telling the larger story you are writing.

✐ **Don't think in terms of** *the order* **but** *an order*. There may be several appropriate orders to organizing your fragments or stories (see Chapter 3)-- each order is dependent on the *themes* (see Chapter 6, Section C) that guide you. For instance, if you want to convey that you worked hard and rose out of nothing to achieve success, you should set a story about being poor next to one about having achieved financial success. This will highlight the relationship and the disparity between these two times in your life. If, however, rags-to-riches is not a theme that particularly interests you, it will seem normal to insert stories between those of your "poor" period and your "rich" times. By distancing these two periods within your manuscript, you will downplay the link between the two.

✐ *Transitions* **will help link your writing** (whether jottings or complete stories) into an appropriate order. Transitions can be as simple as a linking word like *next*, *however*, or *lastly* in front of a paragraph or group of paragraphs, or a phrase like *as a result of this* or *in consequence*.

Other transitions, however, will require additional writing. For instance, your story about yearning to get an education that seemed beyond your reach cannot logically be followed by another about the fine professional-level job you obtained. These two stories need transitional material to show how you overcame difficulties and received the education that prepared you for the fine job.

Generally speaking, a transition is necessary every time a jump in thought or in the sequence of events may not be evident to your reader. As part of your editing process, give your writing to someone to read. If she has to re-read your manuscript to understand how the parts of the stories fit together (as opposed to re-reading because it brought her so much pleasure!), then what you need are better transitions.

Think of your writing as a chain. All of your stories must have a connection to those before and after them or else the chain will not be whole and strong.

C. The active vs. the passive voice

Q. Is there something wrong with using the passive voice?

A. Generally speaking, the passive voice of the verb (the subject has the action done to it) is weaker than the active voice (the subject does the action).

"Mary baked a cake" is active. *Mary*, the subject of the verb *baked*, is doing the action of baking. On the other hand, "A cake was baked by Mary" is passive. Here *Mary* is not the subject. The *cake*, which is *being baked* by Mary, is the subject. The action is being done to it.

"I'm taking a real risk! What if no one likes what I write?" - Workshop writer

✐ **The passive voice has less impact than the active voice.** The reader may experience it as an evasive attempt on your part to not "own" the action of the verb.

✐ **Dependence on the passive voice reveals the writer's own passivity.** She is having difficulty coming to "ownership" of what she is writing about.

"The requirement to wear long sleeves was rejected by the women" is not as strong as "The women rejected the requirement to wear long sleeves". In the passive, the writer does not "own" refusing to wear long sleeves and is hiding behind a "by" phrase. One feels she seeks (perhaps unconsciously) to distance herself from the action.

If you use many passive constructions, ask yourself why. Would using the active voice help you come to ownership of your life and your stories?

Exercise

✔ Select one of your stories that uses the passive voice. Rewrite the story so that every passive construction is changed to an active one.

✔ How does the change to the active voice affect how you feel about the story? Does it give new muscle to your writing-- and your life?

D. The third person

Q. Is it all right to write about myself in the third person, to say "John did this or that" instead of "I did this or that"?

A. Using the third person (he/she) is like using the passive voice. It evades "owning" a story.

It is a useful tool for a person to use when he is working his way through a difficult situation that cannot yet be faced head on: the death of a mate or having been abused or feeling extreme guilt. Using the third person can be a way of beginning to accept what may hitherto have been too difficult to incorporate into one's life. Frequently a *Turning Memories Into Memoirs* workshopper who writes in the third person is rehearsing living with the truth. The third person gives him something to hide behind if the pain begins to assault him.

✐ **Ultimately, as lifewriters, we all need to write our stories in the first person so that the "I" can "own" the life.** Our task (at least in terms of self-growth) will not be completed until we have done so.

"Writing in the third person gave me a place to start. I couldn't have written in the first person right away."
  - Workshop writer

E. Is good grammar needed?

Q. Is good grammar needed in lifewriting?

A. To anyone writing lifestories, I would caution, "Get your story down on paper and don't worry about 'good grammar'-- at least, not at first."

Composing a first draft is more important than producing good grammar. Forget the curmudgeonly high-school English teacher who used to peer over your shoulder; forget your *inner censor*. The correct placement of a comma is not the most important issue in the world, nor is it proof of one's worth as a human being. Your first task is to flow with the prose and get your ideas and feelings written down.

✐ **Grammar, however, plays an important role in writing**. What may sound fine when spoken can become merely dull, repetitive, and inexpressive in writing. In

"I aint never been too good at no grammar!"
  - Workshop joker

The rule against split-ting infinitives is an example of mean-ingless "good" gram-mar. The rule origi-nated in the days when Latin was still dominant in British academic circles. Since Latin infinitives consist of only one word, it was consid-ered more faithful to them to translate them into unbroken English units-- hence no splitting. This is a "good" grammar rule that has nothing to do with present-day North American Eng-lish-- and everything to do with another language of another time.

conversation, we have recourse to facial expressions, voice inflections, pauses, hand gestures, etc., to complete our spoken words. On the page, however, all we have is the writing itself-- and commas, dashes, periods, paragraph breaks. That's why grammar, and the conventions we call correct usage, are ultimately important to you as a lifewriter.

Think of grammar as a code that we agree on to make communications clearer. Periods, commas, capital letters, past tenses, the spelling of words-- all of this is meant to communicate the meaning of a text to a reader who is un-familiar with you and with your story. Good grammar helps us to avoid such foolishness as "I threw the hat over the fence that I was wearing." (How did the fence fit around your ears?) *It is not a matter of "putting on airs" nor of snobbery, but a matter of effective communications.*

Our language experience (especially in its written form) is codified so that both writer and reader can (as much as possible) mean the same thing by the use of the same symbols. You can understand the writing on this page because we both understand the grammar that is in use here-- I, the writer in my office in Maine, and you, the reader wherever you are.

✐ **Within the range of "good grammar", there are many perfectly acceptable-- and different-- decisions.** That's a wonderful thing about grammar that your cur-mudgeonly high-school teacher probably didn't tell you. Where to start or end a paragraph is subject to choice-- *your* choice. The same is true for commas and periods and dashes, and the correspondence of tenses.

Buy yourself a contemporary grammar book to refer to whenever necessary. They are available in many book stores. (I recommend that you avoid your old high school grammar text. Its rules are probably outdated now. Lan-guage is not static; it is always in process.) Confidence will open you up to the flow of language and you'll notice that your writing will become more fluent and fun to do.

When you want to ask, "Do I need to use good gram-mar (or correct spelling)?" try reformulating your question. Ask instead, "Do I need to be understood?"

F. Say it once. Period.

Q. Shouldn't I try to recapitulate my story at the end of it-- just to wrap it up nice and neat?

A. No! Do not repeat the theme or any part of your story in a tag-on summary sentence or paragraph at the end of your piece-- just in case no one got the point! Not only is this unnecessary but it is also an insult to your readers' intelligence and to your own writing ability!

Here is an example. In a piece about a death in the family, the writer *shows* the members of a family mourning together and supporting each other through difficult days. The writer carefully chooses dialogue, image, and detail to reinforce the notion of family solidarity and its benefits. Great stuff! So far so good! Not a dry eye left in the reading audience. The story line has achieved its purpose.

Then, having effectively *shown* this family successfully dealing with its grief, having up to then resisted the impulse to *tell* the reader what to think and feel, the lifewriter concludes: "And so if members of a family support one another in times of adversity, they too can find themselves reinforced, uplifted, blah, blah, blah..."

Well, besides being objectionably preachy and telling rather than showing, *the intrepretative tag-on is simply redundant.* The writer has already made her point through effective choices of various writing techniques. There is actually nothing the recapitulation can tell that her story hasn't already shown more dramatically. (See Section I below for conciseness.)

✐ **Always look at your last paragraph (or two) with an eye to eliminating it.** It is very likely repetitive and dull writing and your story will almost always be improved by striking it out. Always let the story speak for itself!

✐ **Introductory paragraphs in a story are often only warm ups** for the real start which occurs in a subsequent paragraph. Make your start this real first paragraph and leave your warm-up writing where it belongs-- in the wastebasket! You'll be glad you didn't hide your true lead under unnecessary false starts.

"What do I do if no one gets what I'm trying to say?"
- Workshop writer

"I'm having a hard time throwing anything away. I think I'll keep those repetitive last paragraphs in my journal."
- Workshop writer

G. What's verisimilitude?

Q. Do my stories really need to seem real?

A. **Verisimilitude** is that quality in a piece of writing that makes it seem "like the real thing" (*verum* means *true* in Latin and *similis* means *like*). Every story needs a good dose of verisimilitude if it is to be accepted by the reader.

If a movie is allegedly set in France, verisimilitude can be established by showing a *café-terrasse* scene. There will be French spoken in the background. The viewer then can accept the fiction that the story "really" took place in France. If the scene is shot in an apartment with English music on the stereo and an American newspaper on the coffee table, it is much harder for the viewer to accept the fiction that the story took place in Paris. Verisimilitude will be harder to attain (and maintain) not only because the necessary props are missing but also because the clues furnished contradict the fiction of the stated locale.

Your reader willingly makes a compact-- implicit, of course-- with you, the writer. As long as you provide enough clues to make the story seem real, the reader will *suspend his disbelief.* In other words, he'll go along with the idea that the story really happened when, where, and how you say it happened.

In practice, this means that the lifewriter must select appropriate details to reinforce and corroborate the story. If the story is set in 1935, the people have to be doing things people were doing in 1935-- listening to the news on the radio, for instance. Conversely they cannot be doing things people were not doing in 1935-- watching the news on television.

✐ **Establishing verisimilitude in your story does not mean including every detail of a certain time and place.** There are far too many details in your life for you to do that. Were you to include all the false starts and the dead ends-- not to mention all the delicious dinners!-- experienced in life, your story would soon be overcrowded, like a room so stuffed with furniture that people cannot get around easily within it. No, you will need to select carefully what you will include. A few judicious details here and a few others there will do quite nicely-- and will be quite enough if you have chosen well. (Think of the Paris *café-terrasse* where the waiters are speaking just a few well-placed words in French to be overheard in the background.)

The analogy of the tip of the iceberg is *à propos* here. Only ten percent of the iceberg sticks out of the water while ninety percent is submerged. Seeing only the exposed ten percent of the iceberg, a ship's navigator knows what to expect of the floating mountain of ice.

That's the effect to achieve in your lifewriting. By including just the most effective and revealing details, you can use a part to convey the essence of the whole. If you want to show your family's poverty, describe the worn, faded linoleum in the living room. Going on, however, to describe the mismatched chairs in the kitchen and the frayed towels and chipped dishes, blah-blah-blah, begins to be a catalogue of facts rather than a story. (Suddenly the whole iceberg looms out of the water and the reader is overwhelmed!)

✐ **Remember: verisimilitude requires that you steer a clear course** between boring your reader with too many details that may not have any meaning to anyone except you and leaving your reader up in the air because you have not made the story *seem* real to others by including just enough judicious details.

H. Avoid clichés and stereotypes.

Q. Why are clichés and stereotypes ineffective?

A. Clichés and stereotypes place people in categories. They are short-hand ways of writing and speaking that reflect ready-made thoughts. They adversely affect the ways we relate to our families and friends as unique individuals.

"She was a mother-hen-- you know how mothers are!"
"My father had a heart of gold."
"Those were beautiful days when we were happy."

These examples of *clichés* and stereotypes reflect ways of thinking that get in the way of our seeing people as individuals and events as unique. If you think of *your* mother in generic terms of "mother", you will be weighed down with all the sentimentality that second-rate movies, novels and songs sell us. Instead, see her as a person, a woman, who met the challenges of mothering as successfully as she did or could. Do the same with your father. And everyone else in your stories.

And that goes for "youth" and "love" and "family" and everything else that can get real sentimental real fast.

✐ **Beware of words and phrases that have the ring of having been heard elsewhere.** If you sense that a phrase is not your original pairing of two or more words, that you may have "borrowed" it, chances are you have a *cliché* or stereotype dripping off the end of your pen-- gushing out on the paper to embarrass you later!

✐ **Create a language that is as fresh as you are.** The challenge of writing is to have your words reflect you and your story, not someone else's version of you and your story. By using *clichés* and stereotypes, you slip into someone else's version and away from your truth.

I. Be complete and concise.

Q. When have I said enough and when have I said too much?

A. This is one way to write: You write everything you need to write on a topic (*completeness*) and then eliminate all that you can without changing the meaning of the story (*conciseness*). What's left is your story. It's really just that simple.

As you write, keep looking at your prose as a stranger would. Is there enough information to understand what you are trying to communicate? If not, keep adding details. Unless you are very good, very experienced, don't edit at this point. Just let your text flow.

Yes, you are likely to repeat yourself and to include irrelevant information. You might even babble on. But don't hold yourself back. Your writing needs to flow. Every activity in its proper time.

Once you feel you've said everything you have to say, you need to undertake two tasks:

1) **Eliminate everything that is redundant.** Examine your text. Have you said exactly the same thing before (or something very similar)? Choose the most effective version and *delete the rest*. **Saying it once is usually enough.**

✐ **Don't forget the redundancy that creeps in when you have your narrative repeat the dialogue.** Put meaning into the dialogue not into a tag. *She was very hungry. "After not having eaten for days, I am starved," she said.* Have the dialogue carry the meaning here and eliminate the sentence *She was very hungry.*

✐ **Linking phrases can also be redundant.** *Our house in Des Moines was a two story brick building. In comparison, our house in Cincinnati had only one story and was built of wood.* Here the two sentences are obviously a comparison and you do not need the words *in comparison.*

✐ **A third form of redundancy occurs when an adjective attempts to act as a superlative to a word that is itself already a superlative.** Examples of this are: *complete* silence is no more silent than *silence*; a *dead* corpse is not more dead than a *corpse*; *very* sincere is not more sincere than *sincere*; *true facts* are not more true than *facts*.

2) **Eliminate material (even if interesting) that does not contribute to the overall impact you are aiming for within a story.** Writers can find themselves with interesting, well-written material that belongs elsewhere. Sometimes this material can be an excess of description-- remember the tip of the iceberg. Other times, you may have written a story within a story, a separate tale with its own *beginning, middle,* and *end*, its own set of images and characters. It may even be a lovely tale, that will move the reader. Nonetheless, take it out. File the story-within-a-story away for future use. It won't go away-- it'll be waiting for you later. Perhaps it can fit into the flow of your lifestories-- but at a different spot. Or, perhaps you have a lovely description that you need to expand and make into a story of its own.

Michelangelo, when sculpting his statue *David*, is said

to have remarked that he chipped away at the block of stone until the statue emerged. He eliminated all he could and what was left could not bear any more elimination: at last, Michelangelo had the statue that had been waiting for him.

Within the many pages you have written is your much smaller-- and better-- story. *The story you want to end up with is encrusted in excess prose.* Keep chipping away at your text until you can't chip any more without detracting from your story. That will be your *David.*

Your story will then be **complete** and **concise**.

J. Use precise language.

"The difference between the right word and the nearly right word is the same as that between lightning and the lightning bug."
- Mark Twain.
writer

Q. Can you write good lifestories without an extensive vocabulary?

A. An extensive vocabulary can only help you-- if by that you mean many *precise* words rather than many *big* words.

Precise words are specific and not vague like *nice, awful, big, okay. She was nice* is vague. *She had a gift for understanding different points of view* is specific.

He was awfully big is vague. You might write instead: *My father measured six foot three and weighed 200 pounds.*

Don't write: *The job was okay.* Write: *The job was in my field of competence, but its salary was inadequate and its requirements did not challenge me. I felt lucky to have the job, however.*

In each of these examples, I have added meaning where I replaced vague words with *precise* language, but I did not use *big* words. *She was nice* does not qualify *how* she was *nice* nor *what* I understand *nice* to mean as opposed to what the reader might understand *nice* to mean.

Go over your text. Look at individual words. Do each of your words carry full weight or do you have *flabby* words like *nice* and *awful.* If you do, replace them with specific (not necessarily *big*) words and phrases that contribute precisely to your meaning.

In a general way, writers make use of *flabby* words and

phrases because they have not taken the time to explore the depth and breadth of what they are writing about. Like *clichés* and *stereotypes*, flabby words and phrases are lazy forms of writing. They say very little-- when you need so very much to communicate all you have lived!

✐ **Remember:** replace all flabby words or phrases with others that are *precise* and *full of meaning*. You will not be there to notice the confusion appear on your reader's face as she struggles to understand your text. You will not be there to say, "What I really mean is..."

K. The 10% rule:
be more concise!

Q. Do you have a favorite rule to keep in mind?

A. One rule I have often practiced-- and *always* to my great benefit-- is to eliminate 10% of my text.

Even when I think there's nothing left to cut, that my prose is concise and precise, I find I can cut something out. Always.

Think of yourself as a publisher who has space available for only 90% of your text. What can you eliminate without changing the meaning of your lifestory? If you have typed five pages, eliminate half a page. If you have typed ten, eliminate one full page.

"This lifewriting workshop is hard work!"
- Workshop writer

Many writers who published their own work in the days before computers and desk top publishing have written about how typesetting by placing each lead character in a frame and then working with hundreds of heavy frames taught them to value conciseness. Diarist and novelist Anaïs Nin wrote about learning to ask herself whether or not this or that word or phrase was essential enough to warrant the work of being typeset and printed.

Although publication is not such a physical experience today as it was, it is still an expensive proposition. Play the editor who's trying to meet her budget: eliminate 10% of your text!

Lifestories from the Workshops:

Tillie *by Bill Fagan*

At the age of twenty, I had been a stranger in one strange place after another for several years. Now R.G. Blome had invited me to visit during chore time. He wanted me to meet his wife Tillie as well as to be introduced to their Iowa farm. He and Tillie wanted a live-in hired man to replace their son who had recently moved to a place adjacent to theirs to begin his own farm.

Arlo, a friend of mine, brought me. When we drove into the yard just after daybreak on a July day, the dogs barked. Tillie probably wasn't expecting me quite so early. I heard an upstairs window open. She called out to tell me she would be right down. She came so quickly I knew she was up and dressed already. She explained that R.G. would be along soon.

*An engineer, **Bill Fagan** was born in New Jersey and traveled widely as a young man. He has worked at a variety of jobs and now lives in Maine.*

She asked me to follow along to the barn. This small, grey-haired woman, who couldn't weigh one hundred pounds, moved quickly in front of me. She opened a large door to let the cows into the barn. They found their usual stanchions to put their heads into. While Tillie was putting measured amounts of ground feed in front of each cow, she asked me about myself.

I told her I had only just learned to milk cows. My inexperience would be no problem, she said. She did most of the milking anyway. I could be the one who cranked the cream separator. She didn't like doing that.

When she was almost finished with the first cow, R.G. joined us. He didn't milk any faster than I did. One of his hands had been badly injured a few years earlier while he was working at a threshing machine.

After all the cows were milked, we carried the milk to the room where the cream would be separated from it. But R.G. told me that could be done a little later. He wanted me to accompany him to the feedlots to show me how the steers and hogs were cared for and fed each morning. I noticed Tillie carrying a large basket of corncobs into the house.

Half an hour later, when R.G. was about finished with the feed lot chores, Tillie called him, and we went to the house for breakfast. After she had left us, Tillie had built a fire in her cookstove using the corncobs. She had no other fuel for cooking. There was no electricity until several years later. There was no gas, either, so summer and winter Tillie built corncob fires.

She had set three places at the table. In the center were platters of such things as might be expected at dinner. There were fried eggs, ham, sausage, potatoes, home-made bread and toast, butter, coffee and milk, apple pie, and about half of a large chocolate cake. Don't think I have a remarkable memory: this was the usual break-fast, to which sometimes Tillie added hot cereal, oranges, or other fruit.

That's how I started my first day as a "by the month" hired man. I learned what it was like to be part of a family and to be mothered for the first time in my life.

Less than a month later, when R.G. and Tillie took me to her family's annual re-union and picnic, I knew I was no longer a stranger in another strange place.

If World War II had not intervened, I probably would still be there today.

Chapter 9 Keeping It Going and Wrapping It Up

A. Stay with the process.

B. Defend your writing time!

C. Lifewriting groups

D. The finished product

E. Good luck!

A. Stay with the process.

You may already be looking forward to the moment when you hand over an attractive collection of stories to your children, your grandchildren, your relatives, and your friends! It's understandable that you are impatient to reach this stage of your writing-- understandable yet dangerous. Rushing your lifewriting may subvert your whole effort. You may end up with a collection that is only a portion (in quantity and/or quality) of what you could have produced if you had taken your time!

Too early in the process of discovering their stories, some lifewriters yearn for the finished product-- often something that is recognizably a book. They begin typing a final version or binding a manuscript.

Later, they think of something they forgot to include-- something interesting and very important to their story! Because of the amount of "finish" work they have already invested in the look of their manuscript, some writers are reluctant, or even refuse, to do the re-writing needed to insert new material in their lifestories. (If they have used a typewriter, adding new material may mean retyping the whole manuscript!) They settle for what they have-- a finished product that is not the story they and their families deserve.

Don't let this happen to you! Slow down! Linger over your stories: let lifewriting be a process of discovery for as long as possible. Allow yourself to add a little or a lot, to delete a word, a paragraph or a whole section, to change the placement of events and ideas so that emphases change and interpretations become more clear. (Think of lifewriting as a soup that is simmering. Long, slow cooking will produce a tastier meal.)

Lifewriters who approach writing as a process are likely to ask themselves, "What will I learn today?" Their writing sessions will be times of discovery, times of learn-

This chapter will help you to bring your writing to a successful completion.

Often, when you think in terms of a product, usually a "book", you will be burdened with meeting a standard found in "real" books-- usually a standard of perfection. Attaining that standard may be beyond your reach right now. The result? You feel discouraged.

Thoughtful people don't make decisions in haste. Thoughtful writers don't write in haste.

ing, always fresh and tantalizing as their sensibilities, intelligence, and imaginations reveal the workings of their lives to them.

Learn to enjoy this process of inquiring into your past and giving shape to your memories and insights in an appropriate written form. You will work with considerably more pleasure and freedom than if you rush your lifewriting into a final version too soon.

Exercise

✔ Reread those stories which you consider finished.

✔ Have you written as much about the *characters*, the *plot*, the *setting* as you are capable of and as much as you wanted to?

✔ Have you developed your *theme*, your *tone*, and your *point of view* adequately to convey what you wanted to in your story?

✔ Could your stories use the information that you can get only through additional interviews or research?

✔ If you feel there is more to be said in any of your stories, open yourself up to the process of adding to your writing. It may seem difficult now, but it will be even more so in a year or two when you are sorry that you failed to do justice to your story.

B. Defend your writing time!

This is a review section that looks at when you write and the conditions necessary to write.

As you continue to write, maintain an habitual time during which you work. You may have to negotiate with your housemate(s). Do it clearly and on a regular basis. Depending on the scope of your project, they will have to accept a shorter or longer duration of commitment. Open communication about scheduling can protect the success of your whole project by keeping your time available for regular, serious work.

✐ **People with young children do have several options.** One is to place the child(ren) in a pre-school or arrange for other childcare. Parents can also negotiate with their child(ren). Whatever their age, children can learn how to respect a parent's commitment.

Whenever I have said this to people, there have been those who have snickered, "Ha, we can tell you don't have kids!" On the contrary, I have two and have written while caring for them. Like everyone else, children learn to meet the expectations we have of them. Parents whose kids don't allow them any writing time are often parents who are giving their kids an implicit permission to disturb them at work. When kids receive the cue that their parents expect interruptions, kids will then interrupt them-- on cue!

When my own children were still as young as four and even three, they were able to respect those occasions when I needed time to write. Alone in the house with them, I would point to the clock and tell them that when the hands on the clock were in a certain position, I would stop writing and read them a story or go for a walk with them. Meanwhile, I made sure they had their toys available and a snack ready. I told them they could have the snack when the hands on the clock were at a certain place. Because I honored my part of the agreement, my children almost always kept theirs. There were even days when, under pressure of a writing deadline, I wrote both morning and afternoon. Even then, my children respected my need-- but my writing day was interspersed with meeting their needs too: snacks, meals, readings, and walks.

Your children recognize the seriousness of your commitment to many things in your life: your job, your house and yard chores, bill-paying, keeping dentist appointments. It is because you will not put these tasks off that your children accept your commitment to them. Why should lifewriting not be in this category?

✐ **Remember that your expectations are often self-fulfilling.** When others consistently play the role of obstacle to your lifewriting and you consistently fail to overcome the difficulty, you might ask yourself, "Am I avoiding my commitment to writing? Am I using others as excuses and am I unconsciously evading this work?"

Requests we make of others are sometimes not met because we don't expect to be successful. Always approach negotiations with the expectation of success. Ever heard of the self-fulfilling prophecy? Think positive!

When you say, "Mommy has been working too long. She's so sorry you have to interrupt her again", you're telling your child that she may interrupt you. In fact, your child did not have to interrupt. She made a choice based on her experience: interrupting Mommy at this task is permitted.

Exercise

Review the schedule you set for yourself in Chapter 1.

✔ Has it proven appropriate for you? What specific changes would make it a more effective tool for you to use as a successful lifewriter? Decide on necessary changes and enter them on your calendar, inform your housemates, and stick to your schedule.

✔ If the schedule you created earlier remains appropriate, have you been able to stick to it? Have others respected it? What cues have you given (and are you giving) them about how serious you are or are not in maintaining this schedule?

✔ What do you need to change in your environment to make sure that your schedule works for you now and will continue to work for you until your writing project is finished?

C. Lifewriting groups

This section looks at the benefits of being part of a lifewriting group.

A good writers' group can give you invaluable support and see you through to the end of your lifewriting. Regular meetings essentially become deadlines to complete portions of your project. Remember that workshop or group deadlines can be very stimulating (after all, who wants to show up at a meeting and be the deadbeat who hasn't brought any writing to share!)

A group is especially important if your mate or others in your life do not understand what you are doing and are disparaging of your efforts. ("Why don't you just enjoy yourself at your age!" "Why do you want to write instead of going to the Tupperware party!")

✐ **In forming a lifewriting group, the first people to look to are your friends, your relatives, or your mate.** If you don't know anyone who is interested in lifestories, advertise or otherwise "go public" (church bulletin, poster at the grocery store or library, etc.).

If you specifically need the support of people similar to yourself, advertise in a newspaper of your ethnic group, of your vocational background, or of your religion.

If you do advertise in a general circulation magazine, be sure to identify those features that will be important to you in a fellow writer (e.g., women in their 60s).

(The few first times you meet with a group of strangers, you might consider getting together in a safe, public place like a senior center or a library rather than in a private home or apartment.)

✐ **A functioning group may consist of only one other person or of many others.** Establish ground rules (meeting time and place, length of meeting, regular operating procedures) and reassess these rules periodically to ascertain that they continue to meet your needs. Having a structure for your get-togethers will also encourage you to take the group seriously-- even if there are just two or three of you.

✐ **Starting a group is not an effort to make friends.** It is an occasion to meet fellow writers who may or may not become friends. You can learn a lot from people with whom you would otherwise not spend time. Your association is skills-oriented and not personal.

After a few meetings, it will be obvious whether you can or cannot work with a particular group. Remember: you want to learn to write better; you have not come to learn group dynamics or to create long-term strategies to get people involved. Resist the urge to be a missionary, a counselor, or a client. (Review the concept of archetypes discussed in Chapter 6, Section E.) *If the group is not helping you to meet your* **writing goals***, it's not the group for you.* You should quit that group or assess realistically if you can change it to meet your needs.

✐ **Some reasons for a group not working are:** lack of chemistry between participants; too great a difference in education or experience; dependency or other emotional shortcomings on the part of members; discrepancies in members' commitments to writing and to improving themselves as writers.

If the group is not working for you and you are convinced that it is not likely to meet your needs in the future, let members know you will not be continuing to meet with them. It's not easy. I know, I've had to go through that process myself. It's common courtesy, of course, to let people know that you are leaving. It is also good practice

"Sometimes I just had no idea how to be more clear and more detailed. I just didn't. A good thing I had a group. They always came up with suggestions."

- Workshop writer

Being part of a writing group is still a good idea even if your first attempt to get one going isn't successful. Don't throw the baby out with the bath water! Try again.

in openness (a quality essential in the writer). Once you have made your decision to leave, look for or create another group.

✐ **When a successful group has done its work, let it end.** Often, you will know the time has come to disband when usually-regular members begin to miss meetings or keep showing up late. Make a clean finish of it and let members go off on their own-- or, of course, you can continue contact (a social or writing connection) on some basis with whichever members you want!

Exercise

If a writing group appeals to you, take the time right now to assess your needs.

✔ Note how many and what kind of people would be ideal, how frequently you would like to meet and for how long. What public spaces in your community are available?

✔ Reach out to potential group members. Devise a list of people (including librarians and writing teachers who can connect you with other beginning writers) to call or write. Post an announcement, or buy advertising space in an appropriate publication.

D. The finished product

This section looks at how to package your lifestories.

"I wrote an inscription and autographed every copy I gave away. It made me feel like a real writer."
- Workshop writer

Now at last, it's time to consider the finished product!

The record of your lifestory will, of course, contain the narratives this book has helped you to write, but your finished product can also include all sorts of other material that will substantially enhance both the quality and the appearance of your lifestory.

1) **Include photos and photocopies.** It is easy to reproduce old photos and to include them in each copy of your lifestory. You can also photocopy other documents such as birth and marriage certificates, obituary notices, letters, diplomas, children's drawings, etc. Any of these can be set in or near the text they illustrate.

There are now photocopiers which will reproduce your color photographs with remarkable fidelity to the original at a fraction of the price of regular photography. Inquire at quick printers in your area for further information. You will be astonished at how inexpensively you can include good prints in your book.

2) **Include lists of things that don't fit into the narratives.** For example, favorite foods (with the recipes, of course!), favorite songs or hymns (with the words and/or notations or tapes of the songs), novenas and devotions, favorite sayings of a person. Include this material within a chapter (sometimes set off from the text by a "box"-- easy to do with a word processor) or at the end of one. This material can also go at the end of your book as an appendix.

Another very useful list is that of places where someone lived along with a description and/or drawing (or map) of the place as it was then. This is also a good spot to include photos of the place then (and now). This helps your reader to picture the scenes and places you are describing and makes your story more vivid.

3) **A genealogy is a precious addition to any lifestory.** But, creating one is a different enterprise altogether from lifewriting. Genealogical research is demanding and merits that you learn what you can of its methodology. Before you do that, however, be sure to inquire if any distant cousin has done any of that work already.

A chart of the family in the last few generations is also useful for people to refer to. Your children and grandchildren may not remember as clearly as you do the names of Aunt Olga's six children. A chart can spare you the obligation of incessantly placing tags on a character ("My cousin Rita who was Aunt Olga's third daughter and fifth child..."). Genealogical charts are frequently included at the beginning of a story or in an appendix.

4) **Publish your story.** If what you want are ten or so copies, photocopy your collection and bind it in a hard cover that you either make or buy. Local printers can give you a good price for binding ten or more of your photocopied manuscripts. The price for binding small numbers of books tends to be high per copy and would be prohibitive if you were doing a thousand at that rate but is

Leave blank pages at the end of your book as a reminder to your children to take up the writing of family stories for the next generation.

actually very accessible when you consider doing ten.

Decorate the cover with art work: drawings, photos, an embroidery, or a painting.

There are also a variety of soft covers available to you. This is a viable option if your stories add up to only fifty or fewer pages. Soft covers include plastic and poster board with spiral bindings or glued spines. Obviously, if the book effect is what you are going for, these soft cover options are less satisfactory.

Some people want to publish a hundred copies of their lifestories-- or even several hundred. This can be a fairly expensive proposition (price per copy often doesn't drop until after the first thousand copies). If you choose this solution, **do a lot of comparative analysis** before settling on a printer. The prices can vary by as much as fifty and a hundred percent! So do your shopping. Large printing plants with national clienteles almost always offer lower rates (sometimes dramatically so) than small, local firms-- but the disadvantage is long distance communication! (Refer to Poynter and Kremer books in Appendix B: Additional Reading, *Writing-- Technique, motivation, & promotion* for listings of large companies.)

5) **Make your lifewriting resources available to others to work with, too.** Your research notes, information sources, bibliographies, family photos and artifacts, etc. can help others to add their stories to yours to create a fuller family portrait.

6) **Consider donating a copy of your lifestory to your public library or local historical society.** Area residents and history students will appreciate your generosity and your lifestory. More and more, people are aware that history is not only made up of big events but also of the daily lives of people like you and me.

7) **Send me a copy of your lifestory.** Soleil Press will be editing a number of anthologies of lifestories organized around specific themes: e.g., attending a one-room school house; growing up in the 30's, 40's, or 50's; service in World War II; migrating to this country; working in the mills, the mines, the home; etc. I would appreciate the opportunity to consider excerpts from your lifestory for future collections. Send me a copy at the Soleil Press address listed on the last page of this book. (Don't forget to include

return postage if you want your story back.)

Exercise

✔ How you will package your finished product?

✔ What additional information or material will you include in appendices?

✔ Inquire locally about what printing, photocopy, and binding options are available. Check out the same options from large printing houses listed in Poynter and Kremer.

✔ Who will read your lifestory? What community groups will celebrate your accomplishment (even perhaps plan a publication party!) and be grateful to make your lifestory book available to their members?

E. Good luck!

Although we've come to the conclusion of our work together, I hope that this is just the beginning of your exploration of lifewriting and its rewards.

If you think you can succeed, you most likely will.

✐ **Refer to this book often.** It will provide a continuing source of encouragement and motivation to work the magic of storytelling for you and your family.

✐ **Make use of the appendices.** The lifestories gathered in *Appendix A* will provide reassurance and guidance as you continue lifewriting. The reading from the lists in *Appendix B* will broaden and deepen your knowledge.

"I think I can, I think I can, I know I can!"
- Little Engine That Could

✐ **Write, write, write:** that's the most important thing you can do. Be patient; your work and your life deserve it.

Good luck and keep writing!

Appendix A: Lifestories from the Workshops

Our Origins: The Family

Yvette Audet's mémère (l) & family at the train depot.

The lifewriting selections that follow focus on stories of family origins. These sorts of stories are laden with both subtle and overt messages about how to live the lives our families want, and need, for us to live.

As our primary social unit, the family performs a dual task: it acculturizes each successive generation to its methods and styles of survival and growth and then prepares its members to be discharged as adults into a world that will often be unfriendly. To ignore these acculturizing tasks would be to forsake a child's future-- as well as the community's and the culture's.

The readings in this first appendix are excerpts from a few of the many lifestories produced in TMIM workshops.

Many of the stories children are told fall into the category of "founder" stories-- stories centering around an ancestor whose life experience is presented as an example of what it means to be a "real" member of the family. The "founder" can, of course, be a living parent of whom children themselves frequently ask, "Can you tell me about when you were young?"

But, frequently, the "founder" role is conferred on a grandparent or a great-grandparent. When we say, "My grandmother was the kind of woman who...", we are participating in "hero"-making of the "founder". We are taking part, however unconsciously, in the imperative to incorporate and acculturize new family members and to perpetuate our family story by telling how things were done "right" in our family.

Some people may say, "The stories I tell are just for fun-- to entertain my children and grandchildren." Stories are, and should be, fun to tell and hear. But they are frequently more. Looking back on the stories we heard as children, we can see that they contained basic instructions taught us by our families to show us how to behave, to survive, to succeed in the world. In their way, these stories said, "These are the rules for being a member of this family. You will be happier and better for following them."

Each generation reworks, and re-creates, the stories it has inherited from the past to meet its current needs. In this way, the stories of the past-- really someone else's stories-- are adapted to fit into our own self-definitions.

In this section, you will read about Leland Davis' great-grandfather who went away to the Civil War and then traveled to the Washington Territory to be a lumberman. Once there, he sent money back home. This story teaches young Davises that "real" Davis men go off to adventure in the world beyond the home but they should not forget obligations to the family.

Whereas Leland Davis' Great-grandfather Cunningham was compelled to cross a continent to seek adventure (p. 180), Eva Conroy's grandmother Ericksson "cared enough about her children and grandchildren to cross an ocean to be near them in a new land" (see below). In repeating this story, members of her family uphold a model of Ericksson-Nyberg womanhood.

Anyone who is undertaking lifewriting does well to start with stories of family "founders". If we are to understand ourselves, after all, we must understand the families into which we were born-- the group whose examples continue to shape us into our adult lives. As Yvette Gagnon Audet writes of her grandmother (p. 178), "I have seen traits of my grandmother in my own daughters and granddaughters. Her spirit is still alive in all of us."

My Swedish Grandmother by *Eva Conroy*

One day in January, 1920, the Cunard Star Liner docked in the port of Boston and brought a very special person into my life. She was my grandmother Ericksson.

She had left her home in Sweden to come to America to visit her children, two daughters and a son, who were already here. On that day, she was greeted by her children and three people she was meeting for the first time: a daughter-in-law and two sons-in-law. Soon she would meet her twelve grandchildren.

Grandmother had been widowed at a young age. My grandfather had been a mail carrier who became ill and died of pneumonia after delivering mail in a cold rain one day. Grandmother was left with four small children to raise. The youngest was a boy of two, my mother was four, her older sisters were six and ten. Grandmother had a small pension from the mail service, but it was not enough to feed and clothe her family so she worked outside the home. She loved flowers and always took time to plant many around her home. After she came to this country, she would describe her flowers to us in detail.

Grandmother had a sister named Anna who had come with her husband to America for a visit soon after they were married. They liked it here and decided to stay. They had no children. A few years later, when my mother was fourteen, Aunt Anna invited my mother and my aunt to come live with them in America. Now, sixteen years later, Grandmother was joining them.

I was a baby when she arrived. As I grew up, I did not learn to speak Swedish, nor did she learn English. But we seemed to understand each other just the same. I liked being near her. I'd watch her pull cotton thread through a hole in the flowered metal box she had brought with her from Sweden. Her fingers were sure as she crocheted pretty doilies and table runners. Once in a while, she'd crochet yokes to sew onto the cotton slips her granddaughters wore. She seldom raised her voice even on those rare occasions when she felt it was necessary to get the attention of her boisterous grandchildren.

*Born in Massachusetts, **Eva Nyberg Conroy** has written hundreds of pages of family and personal stories in recent years. A former teacher, she is the mother of two.*

I treasure the memories of her days with us. I can see her still, quietly crocheting by the window in her neat dress and apron, her hair combed back from her face into a bun. She had a serenity about her that made me feel she was as happy to be with us as we were to have her.

Grandmother always kept two things near her. One was a small leather-bound book called an *almanack*. It contained Bible quotations and a family history of births and deaths. The other was her passport. Stamped in Swedish on one of the pages were the words, "to the United States of America and back again". But she never went back. Nor can I go back to the years she was with us, though I often return to my memories of her.

I feel fortunate to have had a grandmother who persevered through hard times and who cared enough about her children and grandchildren to cross an ocean to be near them in a new land. I wish I could have told her this in her own language. But maybe the words weren't important. Maybe the feelings were what counted the most.

My Mémère *by* Yvette Audet

My grandmother, Edithe Beaulieu Lizotte, was born on September 4, 1868 in Sainte Agathe, Maine. This small town is on the shore of the Saint John River across from New Brunswick, Canada. She was the daughter of Pierre Beaulieu and Marguerite Lévesque.

As a young woman, *Mémère* came to Lewiston with some friends and worked at the Bates Mill. This was during the 1890s. However, after a time, she returned home to stay with her brother, Damase Beaulieu, in Lille, Maine, which is in Aroostook County. After a few years Edithe met and married Denis Lizotte. They were wed at the church of Notre Dame de Mont Carmel in Lille. Their wedding day was July 31, 1895. My grandmother was twenty-seven, already old to be a bride, and her husband was twenty years her senior. At the time, this difference in age was not so unusual.

Mémère and *Pépère* had five children: Pierre, Marie, Alfred, Denis, Jr., and Marthe. It was the youngest child, Marthe, who was my mother.

When her husband died, Edithe found herself a widow at the age of forty-one. She was determined to succeed in raising her children. She began to take in neighbors' laundry and worked as a housekeeper for Doctor Hammond to bring in extra money. Years later, she remembered this kindly man and his wife who gave her used clothing for the children.

Yvette Gagnon Audet was born in Grand Isle, Maine. A homemaker and mother of six children, she recently learned to type in order to write her lifestory.

Mémère moved to Keegan, Maine, shortly after my parents were married in 1924. She lived on Hillside Street, close to the church, the grocery store, and my parents' home.

As I remember Mémère in the 1930s, she wore a long, ankle-length black dress with black stockings and shoes. She had long white hair which she wore braided into a bun at the back of her head. She fastened the bun with fancy, shiny hair pins. She often sat in the rocking chair on her porch. Sometimes my brother and I would stop to visit her on our way home from school in the afternoons. She would always have a treat ready for us-- homemade bread with butter, or the best molasses cookies I ever ate.

I remember, too, how we used to watch *Mémère* spin yarn on her spindle. I was always amazed at how fast the wool would turn into yarn. *Mémère* would also do fine embroidery, and she knitted and crocheted.

My own mother would often remind us how *Mémère* always did everything to perfection. *"If it's worth doing, it's worth doing right!"* she would say, quoting her mother.

Mémère was a very religious person. She attended *la messe* every day. Once a year in July, she would go to the sanctuary of Ste-Anne-de-Beaupré in Québec for *la Fête de Sainte-Anne*. I can still see her, sitting on a bench by the door waiting for the train to take her and her friends to Canada. She would be wearing her black outfit with her familiar *cloche* and a beautiful brooch.

I was nine years old when *Mémère* first became ill. It was decided that she could not live alone any longer. Therefore, she moved in with her daughter, *ma tante* Marie, and her son-in-law, *mon oncle* Lézime, and their five children.

Mémère's room was at the top of the stairs at *ma tante's* house. I used to visit her often. She slept in a little white iron bed covered with a brightly-colored handmade quilt. Also in this room was a huge rocking chair. There was a small window by her bed.

Mémère chewed Copenhagen tobacco. It came in a small round box. Her spitoon sat on the floor by her rocking chair. The tobacco was as much a treat for her as the bubble gum she handed out was for us.

After a time, *Mémère* got so sick that we weren't allowed visit her as often. When I did see her, she was wearing a flannel nightgown and a chenille robe. Her blue felt slippers had pompons on top. Her long white hair now flowed down to her waist.

Mémère died on September 11, 1943. Back in those days, we mourned people in their own homes. In *mon oncle's* parlor, my grandmother lay in her casket and people prayed by candlelight. She was wearing her familiar black dress and her lovely snow white hair was neatly braided and fastened with shiny hair pins. Seeing her lying there, I felt the need to touch her just one more time. Little did I know at such a young age how cold she would be. To this day, I have not touched another dead body.

I attended the funeral, for which my mother made me a black satin dress with a white collar. In those days everyone wore black to funerals.

It was quite a sad event.

Today I do a lot of sewing and crocheting, and it still makes me think a lot of my mémère. I remember her smile and her long white hair. My handwork, like hers, also has to be done to perfection or I start over, for I remember my *mémère* saying *"If it's worth doing, it's worth doing right!"*

I have seen traits of my grandmother in my own daughters and granddaughters. Her spirit is still alive in all of us.

Great-grandfather Cunningham by *Leland Davis*

Great-grandfather Cunningham was seventy-four when I was born so my first memories of him must have been from the time he was at least seventy-seven or so. I remember that he and his sister seemed to sit most of the day reading newspapers and magazines.

Great-grandfather would sit in the living room in his Morris chair, puffing on his cigar and reading his Boston *Globe*. His sister, Great-great-aunt Fan, would sit near him in her rocker. They both faced the big Round Oak coal stove. Between them was an oak stand on which was placed a table lamp. It had a glass shade that was dark green on the outside and white on the inside to reflect the light from the electric bulb.

My father was a local merchant, and my mother taught in the town grammar school. Because both of my parents worked away from the house, I spent a great deal of my early years with my grandmother who "kept house" for Great-grandfather Cunningham and Great-great-aunt Fan.

Gramp would take me in his lap and tell me stories of his life. He had traveled to the Washington Territory soon after he had been discharged from the army at the close of the Civil War. He had traveled down the east coast of the continent by boat and had crossed the Isthmus of Panama by train. Once on the Pacific coast, he had sailed north to the Washington Territory. There he had worked at lumbering. He told me about the huge logs which he had harvested near Seabeck, a small town on the west side of Puget Sound.

Recently, I found letters he had written to his father describing the rough life in the logging camps. In one letter, he mentioned he was sending $100 back home-- by a friend hand-carrying the sum to San Francisco where the money was to be transferred to Maine by bank.

Gramp didn't tell me much about his experiences in the Civil War, but I do remember one experience he related to me.

It seems in his company there were two soldiers who weren't particularly attentive to cleanliness and personal hygiene. Unfortunately, Great-grandfather Cunningham was given the assignment to get these two cleaned up. Great-grandfather was under six feet tall and a rather slender individual. In addition, he was young at the time, having entered the military at sixteen. Taking this into consideration, he knew his duty could not be carried out by physical force. So, using verbal persuasion and the authority granted him by his superior, he led the two to a creek where he got them to disrobe and wash their clothes. I don't know just how he did it but he also got these two fellow soldiers to scrubbing each other. And so, he accomplished his mission.

Great-grandfather Cunningham was the last living Civil War veteran in our town and for many years he was part of the Memorial Day Services. Gramp died in 1937.

My Grandmother by Dorothy Butler

*At 75, **Dorothy Poulin Butler** graduated from high school in 1989. She enjoys her great grandchildren and is a volunteer in the Foster Grandparents Program.*

I will tell you about my grandmother, Rosalie Cloutier. She was of average height for a woman, but was quite a heavy person. To me she looked as round as a barrel. Both my parents worked in the Lockwood Cotton Mill in Waterville, Maine, so my grandmother took care of me during the day. My parents had a small apartment in the same building so that made it easier for *Mémère* to babysit.

Mémère kept a pan of milk or cream on the cookstove to make a special snack for us. When it curdled, she sprinkled sugar on it. We ate it with a slice of homemade bread and butter. It must have been a form of yogurt. It was so good!

My great-grandmother, *Mémère's* mother-in-law, had lived with my grandparents. She was a full-blooded Micmac Indian. *Mémère* used to tell me about my great-grandmother's relatives visiting her. They would sit in a circle on a blanket, smoking their pipes. Great-grandmother lived to be 103 years old. I sure wish I had known her.

Rosalie had twelve children: six girls and six boys (including Archie who fell in the Kennebec River when he was five and drowned.) A seventh boy was stillborn.

We lived on Front Street near the old Colby College campus, so *Mémère* decided to earn a little money to help out. She did laundry for twelve students-- washing, ironing and mending for the grand price of one dollar per student.

Picture if you can what wash day was like sixty-five to seventy years ago: no automatic washers or dryers in those days. The clothes were scrubbed on a scrub board. Then the white clothes were put in a boiler with hot water and soap and let boil for some time. After this they were put into a tub of rinse water and wrung out for drying. Most everyone had clotheslines but my grandmother always spread her white clothes on the grass to dry. They were sparkling white when she took them in.

When I got a little older, *Mémère* would have me bring some of my girlfriends to her apartment and she would help us make costumes out of different colored *crêpe* paper. Then she would crank up the old Victrola and play dancing music. We would form a chorus line and sing and dance for her. That was her entertainment for the day, I suppose. We must have looked like moving May Baskets!

I was a teenager when she passed away. I felt her near me for a long time.

Mémère's Boarding House by *Patricia Croteau*

Every time I see or read a cookbook, delicious memories seem to surface and a wonderful person and chef comes to mind. She was my maternal grandmother, Marie Athalie Gagné.

This remarkable woman was born in St.-Joseph-de-Beauce, Province of Québec, Canada, on February 21, 1860 to François and Marie Gagné. Her younger years were spent in her native village. She later became a certified teacher in the French Catholic schools in the Province of Québec. In 1879, according to a letter saved and found, while Marie* was still teaching, she wrote to the Sisters of Charity in St-Hyacinthe, P.Q., asking to be accepted into their community. She must have meditated on this subject for awhile, finally deciding that this was not her calling in life. A few years later, Marie met Magloire Bolduc (born March 29, 1859) from St.-Victor-de-Tring. He was a tall, handsome man, very sturdy in both mind and build. He was able to win Marie's heart which led them into matrimony at St.-Joseph-de-Beauce in the year 1888.

Patricia Chaffers Croteau worked for 21 years as a medical technician at Central Maine General Hospital in Lewiston. She is active in the historic St. Peter and Paul's Church and most recently she co-chaired a fundraising committee to preserve and restore it.

At this particular period, (the turn of the century), many *Canadiens* were migrating to the New England states. They were looking for work in the textile mills and shoe factories because they could not support their large families on the farms.

But factory work was not what Marie and Magloire had in mind when they arrived in Lewiston, Maine, soon after their marriage. They rented an apartment house on Lincoln Street directly across from the Grand Trunk Railway Station. They decided that Marie would cook meals to feed the newcomers who came by train.

In those days, Francois-Xavier Marcotte would meet the immigrants at the Grand Trunk and find apartments for them to rent. They, in turn, bought their furniture at *Monsieur* Mar-

---

* *The pronunciation of names, like many other things in Québec, was affected by British colonial domination. The author notes that her grandmother's name, Marie, was pronounced "Mai-ré", a French version of the English "Mary".*

cotte's beautiful store.

And they ate *chez Madame Bolduc* because she prepared the same meals as their mothers and grandmothers had served back home across the border. Some of Mémère's menus included: *pot-au-feu*, crème au caramel, graisse de roti*, pork roast with brown potatoes, or *roti de porc avec patates jaunes, blanc mange, soupe aux pois, fèves au lard, ragoût de pattes de cochon, tourtières* and rice pudding. These were all foods the workers were accustomed to having at home.

Many people had no intention of settling here in *les Etats*, so they left part of their family behind and rejoined them at holiday times, if weather permitted. Even though the trains might be running, traveling was not too easy. Some of the roads were impassable due to snowdrifts. Maine winters also proved to be very rugged and severely cold.

Mémère had a good clientele. Many local doctors and professional people ate at her table and, since she did most of the cooking, *Pépère* helped with the dishes when he was not working. He sold sewing machines at Provost and Vincent's Import and Retail Furniture Store on Lincoln Street and drove a "public carriage" stationed at 127 Lisbon Street.

In 1891, a beautiful daughter named Marie Berthe Imelda made her appearance. She had the misfortune of being brought up as a single child (see cover photo). Marie and Magloire lost two infant sons: Joseph Emile, born September 3, 1889, and died September 7, 1889; the second, Joseph Aurélius lived from December 25, 1892 to January 23, 1893.

Berthe attended parochial school locally until the age of ten, then studied in Canada at the St-Hyacinthe Convent with the Sisters of the Presentation of Mary until she finished high school. There she was very happy, learning the fine arts of drawing and painting, piano, organ, calligraphy (which was called *la ronde*), keeping a journal, composition and writing-- which made one of her teachers remark: *"N'oubliez pas qu'il n'y a pas seulement l'écriture. Il y a aussi la vaisselle et le ménage dans la vie."**

Following her schooling, Berthe taught third grade at St. Mary's School in Lewiston. She was also a very accomplished musician and shared her gifts with local groups.

One of *Mémère's* boarders at that time was a young eye-ear-nose-and-throat specialist called William Henry Chaffers who had recently (1912) opened his office in the College Block, on the corner of Chestnut and Lisbon Street. He, too, was musically inclined and loved to play the violin. Needless to say, Berthe and William formed a perfect duo, spending many evenings (or as many as a doctor could), with this kind of entertainment. They fell in love over sweet and sour notes from the piano and the violin while getting acquainted.

Berthe was then working for Metropolitan Life Insurance Company where she had replaced Alice Roux who married Gédéon Croteau on September 23, 1912. Alice and Gédéon were later to become my own mother- and father-in-law (see *Black Saturday* p. 91).

Berthe and William were married June 1, 1914. My mother and father enjoyed a honeymoon at the Copley Plaza and had a grand time visiting Boston. They returned to their love

---

* *"stew, caramel cream, roast fat, ..., or pork roast with yellow potatoes, cornstarch pudding, pea soup, pork and beans, pig's foot stew, meat pie."*

* *"Don't forget that there is not just writing in life. There is also dish-washing and house-cleaning."*

nest at 190 Pine Street which had been all set up before their marriage. They owned the three apartments, bought all of their furniture, and decided to raise a family. At this address were born Joseph William Oliver, Hélène Berthe Imelda, Gerald James Maurice, and Clarence.

In 1919 on October 23rd, the family of six moved to the Bradford Peck home at 506 Main Street. *Mémère* and *Pépère* moved in and helped with the increasing family. *Pépère* did a little farming, caring for the cow, for we needed plenty of milk, and the horse which my father rode for exercise and relaxation.

In 1921, along came Patricia Marguerite Irene, then followed Marie Madeleine Rachel in 1923 and Marie Pauline Thérèse in 1926. Seven being a lucky number, the family was complete. We were one big happy family with 11 people in a 14-room house until *Mémère* and *Pépère* needed care that Berthe could not give. So they both became residents of *l'Hospice Marcotte* (Marcotte Nursing Home)where they lived for two years and passed away one week apart. *Pépère* died January 27 and *Mémère* died on February 4, 1929. We were sad to lose our grandparents. Fortunately, my parents were avid photographers and took movies. They kept everything; we have many mementos for our future generations.

The Child is Parent to the Adult

Gloria

Margaret Littlefield Clements about a year before the birthday party.

The stories we remember about ourselves tell us a lot about how we think-- or how we prefer or need to think-- about ourselves.

A particular memory (often of very mundane things or events) survives in the oblivion that has engulfed much of what else occurred in our lives. Why this memory and not another?

Perhaps it is because this memory of an event or an interaction strikes an emotional chord that has continued to be played all our lives-- either to our comfort or dismay. Perhaps the memory calls for an archetypal response we have not yet been able to make to our satisfaction.

For many writers, lifewriting becomes an opportunity to gain an insight, or make a response, that finally puts a conclusion to an event-- sometimes an event that transpired many years earlier! Three-quarters of a century before she took the TMIM workshop, Roseanna (p. 52) had watched her father's funeral *cortège* leave the railroad station of their little town. When she spoke about it to us, she said, "Years afterwards, the sound of a train whistle would make me feel sad." As she read her story to the workshoppers, the pain of her memory overcame her and she wept.

Perhaps, for many of us, memories corroborate a family myth and, in repeating them, we are not only affirming our wish to survive but our bonds to the family itself. We are reinforcing our belonging to a group that will, we hope, protect us from the world at large. Or perhaps the very opposite is true. In writing about a memory, we may hope to end the family's hold on us-- whether it is a strangle hold or just a lingering apron string.

Margaret Clements, for instance, concludes her excerpt that follows thus: "Maybe I retained a little of my childhood resentment from that birthday party day because uncovering this information gave me a real thrill of triumph!"

The stories in this section delve into the first years of the writers' lives. What the writers share with us is a world so different from the one we live in today that many readers may feel the stories are of another culture altogether-- as indeed they are. Like all cross-cultural experiences, they put into perspective our own cultural assumptions.

As children, a large percentage of the writers in the *Turning Memories Into Memoirs* workshops lost one or both parents. The single-parent family we attribute to a phenomenon of the last thirty years-- due in the modern instance to divorce-- seems almost to have been a normative family unit for many people of an earlier generation. But it was death, not divorce, that decimated these families.

There are other differences between then and now of course, the grip of poverty being high on the list as well as the dominance of work-- hard, unrelenting, and frequently not sufficiently lucrative-- in the youths of these writers.

In this section, lifewriters share with us the foundations of their lives, the times when they learned "the rules". It is an experience we all have had.

The Birthday Party by *Margaret Clements*

My mother's maiden name was Nickerson. She was ninth in the line of descent from William Nickerson, who landed in New England in 1637 where he quarreled with the Pilgrims, the King's agent, the General Court and, as one author* said, he kept "in fighting trim" by quarreling with his own family. It should be noted in his defense, however, that he got along famously with local Indian tribes and that he and a nearby chief were good neighbors and good friends for as long as they lived.

My mother herself had a very calm disposition, and I seldom saw her upset about anything. But when I became unruly, sulky, or had a tantrum, my father always said it was a "Nickerson spell". He thus implied that his own family was more amiable, and was able to tease my mother, while I came to accept having my brattishness dignified with a name.

When I was young, week days were dominated by the work ethic, and most social occasions were held for adults, usually in the evening when I was put to bed. Thus, it was a great event in my life when Gladys Moody, a little girl who lived about two miles away, was to be given a birthday party by her mother and I was invited. I remember it vividly.

I wanted to wear my "best" dress, which was an elaborate creation of ruffles and lace since my mother was an expert seamstress. Mother said we would probably play outdoor games and this dress would be inappropriate. We finally settled on a plainer costume. She tied a big bow in my hair, my father harnessed the horse, and I was taken to my first party.

The young guests assembled in the living room, where the gifts were opened immediately, thus eliminating any suspense. I had brought Gladys a pretty china mug, a container then thought proper for a child's milk, called cambric tea*. I looked on somewhat enviously as the other packages were unwrapped. Then we were ushered outdoors by Mrs. Moody and her older daughter who, at fourteen or fifteen, seemed completely grownup to me.

Margaret Little-field Clements was born in Melrose, Massachusetts, in 1905. She was given the Ethel K. Roche Prize for the best short story at the Eastern State Normal School in 1923. A school teacher and mother of ten, she "has been much too busy" to write again until she undertook her lifestories in a TMIM workshop.

We played tag, which I knew about (but was not very good at since I was fat and slow) and then hide-and-seek, which all children know so well. I got scratched and disheveled, hiding in the lilac bushes. I lost my hair ribbon, but it was retrieved by the big sister and tied on my topknot again.

We then played drop-the-handkerchief, which was completely new to me. I needed instructions and corrections, but I soon thought it was a great game. Next, Gladys proposed another game which I had never heard of, but which I later learned was a sort of elimination procedure in which the last player is a kind of goat and subject to ridicule by the others.

Mrs. Moody quite rightly decided it would make some child unhappy and said "no".

---

* *Scott Corbett, "Chatham," in* Cape Cod's Way.

* *Cambric tea is a children's drink: hot water with milk and a bit of sugar in it.*

Gladys persisted. Her mother again refused.

Whereupon Gladys shouted, burst into tears, ran to the outhouse, and locked herself inside. It was only after a good deal of coaxing and cajoling that she emerged, and we all went into the house for birthday cake and lemonade.

Presently an accommodating parent with a double-seated wagon appeared and delivered us all to our homes.

My parents and my grandmother, who lived with us, were eager to hear all about my afternoon. I held their rapt attention with my account of the party until I revealed, "And Gladys had a Nickerson spell!" This announcement was greeted with explosions of laughter. It was then explained to me that "Nickerson spells" were reserved as a family trait, and Gladys, not a Nickerson relative, was exempt. I felt a good deal of resentment about this, and I did not like being laughed at. I felt quite certain that I was not to be blamed for my ignorance.

Many years later, I became interested in genealogy and I found through my research that Gladys' grandmother had been Melvilla Smart, daughter of Miles and Mary Smart. Miles Smart was a grandson of Winthrop Smart whose wife was Rebecca *Nickerson*. Melvilla had married a Captain Ellis, grandson of Manoah Ellis and Sarah Eldridge. This Sarah was directly descended from William Nickerson's daughter Elizabeth. Thus Gladys had as many-- if not more-- Nickerson genes than I did and was rightly entitled to a "Nickerson spell".

Maybe I retained a little of my childhood resentment from that birthday party day because uncovering this information gave me a real thrill of triumph!

Boyfriends by *Mary Everhart*

I went to school in a small Ohio country town surrounded by dairy farms. It was a four-room school, two grades in each room. I liked the idea because after I had my first-grade work done, I could listen to the second-grade lessons. Of course, that made it rather boring in the second grade because I had already learned those lessons.

> *Mary Davis Everhart was born in Ohio and raised two sons. She now volunteers in the Foster Grandparents program.*

We had a lot of fun at recess and during our hour-long lunch period because we had a huge playground-- acres and acres, although there was not a swing or slide in sight. We made our activity schedule according to the season. There was football, softball, field hockey, rope-jumping, foot races, fox-and-geese, London Bridge, and so forth.

The boys and girls were mostly from the surrounding farms and were accustomed to the girls working as hard as the boys, so when it came to choosing up sides for a game there was equality of the sexes. If you could play well enough, you would be chosen-- boy or girl. The only exceptions I remember were the games of jacks which was strictly for girls and mumble-de-peg which was for boys only.

There were no school buses for us in 1923, and since I lived on the opposite end of town from the school, I had to walk. When there was a lot of snow, my next door neighbor, Melvin Thomas, would carry me on his shoulders until we got to my cousin Donny Wolf's house. Then Donny would carry me. Fortunately, I was small for my age!

When I was seven years old, I didn't think about boyfriends of my own, but I loved to go next door and watch my "grown-up" friend, Mabel, prepare for a date with her boyfriend. They went to dances every weekend, and she wore pretty dresses and long strings of beads.

Mabel had beautiful red-gold hair with, of course, little "spit curls" in front of each ear. Before she left, she would always comb and brush my hair, put a dab of powder on my nose and a spot of perfume behind my ears.

One day the matter of boyfriends became a first-, not second-, hand matter, and I put what I had learned from Mabel into use. There was a scuffle outside our door. My aunt opened the door quickly and there were Dale Bucklew and Arlie Latham, rolling on the ground punching each other and shouting something awful. Aunt yelled at them to stop and demanded an explanation. Well, it seems they were delivering newspapers together and Dale said he would bring the paper to our door because I was *his* girlfriend! Arlie said, no I was *his* girlfriend.

Aunt collected the paper from their bag herself and said to me, "Which one is your boyfriend, Mary?"

"I didn't know I had one," I replied, " but if I have to choose, I'll take Dale because he has curly brown hair, and Arlie wipes his nose on his sleeve!"

The Friends of My Childhood: Gloria

by Blanche Pouliotte

When I was eleven, my family moved yet again. This time we located on King Street in Waterville. It meant we belonged to a new parish. Notre Dame had its own school. New parish, new school, new friends. Our neighbor's daughter was my age, and she, among all the rest, became my bosom buddy, the most kindred spirit of all. Her name was Gloria Roy.

Gloria had many talents. She had a good singing voice; she could play the banjo and the guitar and the piano, too. It seemed all her family were musically inclined. She taught me how to play the Hawaiian guitar, which I enjoyed until I was eighteen, when I thought I was too grown-up to play it any more.

Gloria learned to dance from me. Although the Charleston was out of vogue by 1931, I still loved to do it so I taught it to Gloria. I also taught her the few other dances I had seen and learned on the stage during my experience in the "1930 Revue". She and I put on shows for the neighborhood kids. We became very popular that summer.

Gloria had a lovely backyard in which we could play. We made costumes out of newspaper by folding them over and over and then cutting them in strips. They came out looking like grass skirts which we tied around our waists with belts. We danced and sang on the lawn in our costumes. In no time, the yard would be filled with paper.

We played jackstones, we skipped rope, we played house with the two five-year-old girls who lived nearby. We ran races with other kids, we played nuns dressed in Ursuline habits that we put together somehow. We skied on top of the *chaumière** reserved for the dead across the street from the Grove Street cemetery. Gloria loved to skate, but I could never manage due to my two flat feet. We had other friends who joined us in our play, but Gloria and I were always inseparable and very special to each other.

At age 56, Blanche Doucette Pouliotte shared one of the most important days of her life with her husband, Roland, seven grandchildren and two of their children. That day, she received her bachelor's degree from the University of Maine. She enjoys traveling, the theater, genealogy, and lifewriting.

Gloria and I were in the same class at Notre Dame. We often did our homework together. I had better grades in school than Gloria, so I was able to help her with her schoolwork.

We had read about *Sainte Rose de Lima* in our school text. Because Saint Rose had professed a vow of chastity, she splashed acid on her face so men would not consider her pretty enough to marry. We thought we should do the same-- not splashing acid, mind you, but taking the vow of chastity. A vow seemed easy enough for us to do.

We discussed our idea with our friend, Yvette. If we made the vow, she told us, we could *never* get married. What a disappointment! We wondered a moment if Yvette knew something we did not. Then we remembered that Yvette went to public school, after all-- what did she know about chastity?

We continued with our plans. We would wear white dresses and veils, white stockings and shoes, and carry our beads and prayer books in our hands. We approached Mother Sainte-Armande, our favorite teacher. We talked to her about our vow, and she smiled. We should consult our parents, she told us, before we did anything as important as taking a vow of chastity.

My father was a very sick man that summer. He was trying to recover from a double surgery he'd gone through in February. He had cancer, and he had only a few months to live. My mother came with me to talk to him about my plan. With both of them there in the bedroom, I poured out the news that I wanted to make a vow of chastity. My father did not look too surprised-- he knew me very well. My mother looked away quickly with what I thought was a grin. My father told me very seriously that the vow was a worthwhile goal for a young girl four hundred years ago, but it wasn't fashionable any longer. And yes, chastity really did mean not being able to get married. There! Yvette was right!

I was already noticing boys. I had dreams of someday being married and having chil-

---

* *"white-washed cottage"-- here the term refers to a mausoleum.*

dren. So this was disturbing news! I could not understand why I could not make a vow of chastity and have a family too! Papa said I should wait until I was sixteen and then I could make up my mind.

Sixteen was four years off-- a long time to wait!

My father died that July. Where my childhood had been free with a whirlwind of activities, it now turned sober. My mother would not allow me to run around and play as I had before. I was sent to my brother's farm where I could romp with my nephew and nieces if I wished.

In September, my family moved back on Water Street. I did not see Gloria as often as I had before, although we continued for years to visit. We were still dear friends, but we were never the same fun-loving little girls. Nor were we as sure of ourselves. Life had taken a turn.

When we both married (yes, we'd given up on chastity!), her Marguerite and my Charlene were friends. Both our girls could play the piano and sing well. They were in the same class at school. One was dark and the other was blonde, like Gloria and I had been. Yet, somehow they never became as good friends as their mothers had been at their age.

I was not able to talk to Gloria about our girls' friendship. Gloria was gone by then-- she passed away at thirty-three. She had had a bad heart for years, and one day she had a massive heart attack.

She died Christmas week. That holiday was a sad one for me. I tried to keep a bright face for my children, but when they were in bed, I went to pay my respects to my old friend. My best friend!

Ink on my Dress by Carol Gagné

In East Monmouth, Maine, all eight grades were taught in the one-room school house. I was scared to start school. There were big kids there, and I knew hardly anyone except my own brothers and sisters.

We had to walk a mile to school and sometimes, when the road crew hadn't plowed the road with the horse team and plow, we would walk in the fields. In the spring, the roads were so muddy we had to wear boots well into May.

The year I started sub-primary, there were no other kids my age. The teacher couldn't take much time with one student so I was taught along with the first graders. The next year, I was taught some of the second-grade material, and helped with the first. This went on until I was in the sixth grade and a boy my age moved into town. Then two girls who joined us from South Monmouth, so all of a sudden there were four in my class.

The big kids had desks with ink wells to use, but the

The mother of three, Carol Smith Gagné still lives in her native town of Monmouth, Maine.

younger ones didn't have any ink in theirs. One day, when I was still one of the younger ones, there was a big boy shooting spit balls. He got caught by the teacher. She made him swap seats with me so she could keep her eye on him. I went to sit at his desk.

This desk, like all the others in the back, had ink in its bottle. Because I had never had any ink at my desk, I was very curious.

In the process of investigating, I upset the ink and some of it dumped into my lap. There wasn't much in the bottle, but it was enough to make an awful mess.

School was nearly out for the day. I wrapped my sweater around my waist-- glad that Mama had made me wear it that morning. I was some scared of what she was going to say. I had only one school dress, one play dress and one Sunday School dress.

As I was going out the door, the teacher told me, "Carol, you'd better put that sweater on. There's a chill in the air."

I said I was warm enough and hurried home. Mama was out in the garden digging potatoes for supper. I hurried inside to take my dress off and put it in the rinse tub. I had to go to the well to get water, as there was none in the pail by the black iron sink. I ran back to the well and got a pailful. As I came through the door, Mama's voice nearly scared me out of my shoes. "What are you lugging all that water for?"

I told her. And she didn't act mad or anything. She just said I would have to go down to Leah's house and see if she had any two matching grain bags* and to hurry home so I could help with supper.

This meant I had to tell Leah, too. So down to Leah's I cried all the way. The whole world would probably find out I had been fooling around with the ink at school!

When I got back from Leah's, Papa was home, ranting and raving because supper hadn't been started. I hurried to set the table and he went to the barn. Mama said Papa didn't have to know I had ruined my school dress. She would try to find time to make me a new one for Sunday School and I could wear my Sunday dress to school. Things would be all right.

Coming of Age: Adolescence

For most of the writers whose stories appear here, an adolescence of fifty or sixty years ago was not a time characterized by the freedom, leisure, and disposable income that many teens now take for granted. Rather, as these stories tell, the demands and responsibilities of adulthood simply began years sooner than they do today.

Most of the lifewriters in this book were not the offspring of the professional or middle classes-- and as such they reveal the working-class composition of small-town and rural North American society between the World Wars.

Often, as these writers recall their adolescence, they remember-- usually without self-

---

* *a ready and inexpensive source of fabric in those days*

pity-- a time when their younger selves realized that school, and the possibility of job advancement, was indeed limited. Still young, many settled down to low-skilled, low-paying work and soon started families. As one lifewriter stated, "When you'd been taking care of babies since you were nine or ten, it wasn't hard to think of having your own at eighteen."

A number of TMIM lifewriters have fondly remembered being students in small country schools-- but the eighth or ninth grade served as the endpoint for their formal educations.

Others, a smaller number, had a different experience. A mentor, a special person who offered a different modeling than did the family, actively helped them to go beyond their expectations. In this section, we read how Myrtle Hierl's grandmother (see below) made it possible for her to get a high school diploma. Earlier, we read about how Dortha Faulls (p. 73) met a Sunday School teacher who changed her life.

The Depression was in full swing during these years. For many lifewriters in this book, it did not mean a plunge into sudden and utter impoverishment but simply prolonged the poverty their families had always known. It meant going to work-- any work-- and doing without further education.

The effects of the Depression, however, were attenuated by where they lived. In towns or small cities, often-large families could feed themselves from gardens and keep cows, chickens, and pigs without today's zoning restrictions or complaints from neighbors.

As Joseph Croteau wrote (p. 91), "We managed to live through it." His is a stoicism that seems to have characterized many in North America between the wars, whatever their ethnic or religious inheritance. It followed them into adulthood and one suspects that the updated family stories of succeeding generations will contain a fair amount of stoicism-- or reaction to it-- as future writers recall *their* own family stories.

The Gagnon Family, Keegan, Maine, 1945.   *The Gang: Jeannette (l), & Blanche (r), '36.*

Too Young, Too Poor, Too Smart by Myrtle Hierl

At an early age, I learned that I shouldn't just let things happen to me as I grew. I should set goals and work hard to achieve them. The goal I set for myself was to earn a high school diploma. No one in my family had ever completed high school.

I had walked very early and was running around as fast as a weasel, but I hadn't yet said a single word. I was already two years old when my anxious parents took me to a doctor. I had been having convulsions almost four times a day. The doctor took one good look at me, shook his head, and told my folks that I would be retarded for the rest of my life.

Myrtle Black Hierl continues to write, having set herself a schedule for realizing her writing goals.

Needless to say, my next few years required constant care, and my brother became a favorite because he was a normal child. He was enrolled in school and was doing nicely. My grandfather and father were both working for the Foxboro (Massachusetts) Welfare on the road gangs. Once a week my brother would pull me along in a little red cart when my mother would stand in long lines with a lot of other people, just like us, waiting for the bare necessities Welfare gave out.

No one knows how it came about, but suddenly I began to talk in whole sentences. Everyone said it was a miracle from God. My grandmother was very religious and used to read to me from the Bible. She taught me to read and spell this way. And she taught me that my guardian angel is always with me, watching over me.

From the beginning, I knew I was different. Grammie was fond of telling me that I was "special", and also that I was strange. I thought so, too. I seemed to be able to recall things about my early childhood, from an early age. I didn't know how I knew the things I knew, or why.

In September 1929 I began my schooling. I amazed my teacher with my ability to learn how to read, write and spell.

My father and mother both obtained jobs at the Foxboro Company, he as a mechanic and she as a solderer on one of the assembly lines. Eventually, they managed to save up enough money to buy a small farm in Waldoboro, Maine. We left my grandparents' home and settled down back in Maine.

I was a very quiet and introverted child who now had to enter a new school with children of all ages and sizes. It was a one-room schoolhouse with a woodstove in the center of the room. School was dominated by the teacher, Miss Orff, who could be as gentle or as severe as the circumstances required. She taught the proper subjects to each class-- first through eighth grade-- by moving from group to group.

My brother was entered in the second grade class; I was assigned to first grade. James did not adapt well to the change in home and friends and in our school environment. But I was enraptured by all the new and interesting changes. I devoured all that was going on around me in that schoolroom. When James advanced to third grade, I went on to second.

Then James went to fourth, and I went to third. Then half-way through third grade, I was doing so well in my schoolwork that Miss Orff moved me into the fourth grade with my brother. We began the next year together in the fifth grade. But again at the half-way mark, I was moved up. Poor James lost interest in school because his sister, who was supposed to be a "slow learner", was going on ahead. It was hard for him to accept this.

In the meantime, my father's farming wasn't successful. We went back to Foxboro and moved in with my grandparents. Soon, my father went to work as herdsman for a dairy farmer in Westwood. His pay was $100 a month and "found". That was the word for furnishing a home and other benefits-- utilities, milk and farm foods.

That was all well and good for my parents, but for James and me, it meant more changes in school. My brother chose an agricultural trade school in Walpole, while I enrolled in junior high in Dedham.

Life seemed to go smoothly for a couple of years until my father's boss lost his money in the stock market. We were forced to move to another farm job in another town. In the next three years, Dad went from job to job on farms in Mansfield, Natick, Norwood and other towns. I attended different schools, and my classmates were strangers. My brother moved into a boarding home on a farm where he worked with the ducks. My grandmother urged me to stay with her and finish my senior year at Foxboro High School. So at fifteen, I settled in with Grammie and Grampie and faced the pressure of yet another new school. I buried myself in my school work.

Now there came yet another big cloud on my childhood horizon: my classmates snubbed me. They thought I was too young, too poor, and too smart. Oh, how they taunted me! And they were the people I wanted to please more than anybody else! Again and again I tried to make friends to no avail. Finally I decided I couldn't care less. I dove into my schoolbooks and consoled myself by having a close comradeship with Grammie and Grampie.

Graduation was my goal. At last the big day arrived. In cap and gown with all the other students, I endured the pomp and ceremony. At last it was time to take our turns filing up to receive our diplomas as each name was called. When my graduation diploma was pressed into my hand, I recalled the poor years, the years of struggle and change to reach this point. I had succeeded-- no matter how many obstacles I had encountered, I had overcome them.

I was very proud when I joined my parents in the auditorium for their congratulations. Their happiness shone in their eyes as they hugged me, and it all seemed so worthwhile.

That was the end of my childhood.

Potato Picking: A Dollar a Day by *Yvette Audet*

In Aroostook County, in northern Maine, September was potato picking time. All able-bodied men, women and children would go to the potato fields. I was only ten years old the first time I picked potatoes. My brothers and sisters who were old enough and my father would pick potatoes.

We had to get up before sunrise, have a good breakfast of oatmeal, toasts, and good hot chocolate. We also had to get dressed real quick. My mother sewed thick knee patches on our farmer jeans and, under these, we wore long underwear. At least two pairs of woolen stockings went inside our rubber boots. We wore a flannel shirt and wool sweater with a winter jacket on top, head kerchief, and brown cotton fleece gloves.

The farmer we picked for was Mr. Chase. He sent some of his men with a big truck to bring us to the fields. Sometimes these fields would be an hour or more away, so we'd leave our house in the dark, and it would be light by the time we got there.

There would be a frozen crust on the dirt in the rows. Oh, was it ever cold! The farmer was already there when we arrived. He pulled the potato digger with his great big horse. (This farmer had a medium-sized farm; he didn't own a tractor.) Each picker would get a straw basket. They came in different sizes: small, medium, and large. The large size held a peck. I would use the small size. Before we started picking, each section was measured out with sticks as markers.

Some people picked potatoes bending over, some kneeling. If you started out bending over, you'd just kneel down when your back started hurting. I always picked on my knees.

When our basket was full, we would dump it in a barrel. Each picker had tickets of a different number and color. We kept these in our pockets and put one on the top side of our barrel when it was full.

At noon we stopped for lunch. My father would build a fire with dry branches. Everybody would gather around. It was a pleasure to have the warmth. Our mother had prepared us a lunch in the morning. In a big five-gallon yellow tin pail with a big handle, she would have packed lots of bologna sandwiches, cookies, apples, and a thermos of hot chocolate. We also brought a jug of water because we would get really dry sometimes with all that dirt being blown in the wind. Sometimes we would put potatoes in the fire and enjoy baked potatoes.

If we needed to go to the bathroom, we had to go in the woods.

We went back to work at one o'clock and picked until sunset. We rode home on the flat bed of the truck that was carrying the barrels of potatoes to the potato house. After the long ride home, we were so tired we just washed up and ate supper. Ma always had a warm supper ready for us. We would eat and say our prayers with the family and then go straight to bed. Nobody had to tell us to go to bed, we just went!

The picking went on for three to four weeks, depending on the weather. We were paid on Fridays. If I made a dollar a day I worked really hard. My father would count all the money on pay days. At the end of the harvest, this money was spent on winter clothes and some on school supplies. My mother would buy a lot of fabric. She made most of our clothes. She was a hard worker. She would sew until midnight, lots of times.

We all did our share. We were ten in our family. We had wonderful parents. They showed us how to work and share. We all learned give and take a lot.

Waitressing: the Worster House and Christmas Cove

by Irene Hathaway

When we graduated from Maria Clark Grammar School, my classmates and I really felt all grown up. To think-- in the fall, we would enter our new high school! It was in Hallowell, down the corner of Central and Warren Streets, right across from where I lived.

That fall, I got a job as a waitress at the Worster House in Hallowell for what they called "dinner" (we had always called it "supper"). The new waitresses had to train very hard for the job, as Mrs. Fred Worster herself took care of the dining room. She was the owner.

Irene MacQuarrie Hathaway is now retired. Married in 1931, she is the mother of one son who is a medical doctor with the rank of colonel in the US Air Force.

We would go every day after school for our lessons on how to wait on tables the correct way. First, we had to learn how to set a table, then which side to serve the food from. After that, we had to make sure our silver was cleaned after every meal, glasses washed and put upside down on the sideboard, as well as finger bowls, which we must always remember to serve when the meal was finished. The final touch was the fancy dish of mints and nuts to be placed on the table.

Mrs. Worster was a wonderful teacher. We sure worked hard to please her, and she had a lot of patience with us. She taught us how to stack our plates and serving dishes on the big trays and how to stack the empty ones to go back to the kitchen.

The chef, Mr. Noyes, had charge of the kitchen. He was very nice to me. He knew I didn't get any pay, only tips. As a friend of my family, he also knew we needed the money, and business was slow at the Worster House in the summer.

Mr. Noyes went down to Christmas Cove to work in the summer and he asked me and my sister, Louise, to go with him. I talked to Mrs. Worster; she said to go and I would have my job back in the fall.

Louise and I packed our things and away we went to the most beautiful spot on the ocean. It was a breath-taking piece of land that juts out into the ocean. The Inn was very large with a veranda on the three sides that faced the water. Also there were a small store and two large dorms for the help.

The Inn catered only to wealthy people. Some came for a month; some, for the season. Once people chose their table, it was theirs for the length of their stay. We waitresses got small wages, but when people went home, they left us good tips-- boy, did we feel rich! There wasn't much place to spend it, so our friend Mr. Noyes took care of our money for us.

Now we didn't have a dull moment. Some of the help came from all around the area, some from college, and we were all a big family. We got along especially well; our various ages didn't make any difference. After work, we would all get together and head for the rocky coast. Sometimes we would build a fire, and have hot dogs and marshmallows. Two of the boys brought their guitars, and we would sing until the ten o'clock bell rang. That meant *head for the dorm*.

The Inn had a casino for the guests, and every two weeks we could use it. We would get someone to play the piano and the guitar. We sure had a ball, but again at ten o'clock, we had to head back to the dorms. I met a very nice fellow who went to the University of Maine. As the season came to a close, we said our goodbyes. We were all together for four summers. It was sad at the end, as we knew we wouldn't all be back again.

Later, we all got a letter from Hazel, who lived in New Harbor. The Inn had burned flat, including the dorms and the store. We all wrote to one another for a while. Then our correspondence dwindled to Christmas cards. Then those stopped, too.

But what a marvelous four years we had at Christmas Cove! It's a wonderful memory.

The Friends of My Childhood:
Jeannette by Blanche Pouliotte

I had quite a few friends in my teens. Jeannette came close to being one of my very best friends. We attended Waterville High School together. After school, we frequented movie houses, went on picnics at the lake, and we had parties as often as possible.

There were no school dances at Waterville High in those days before the combination auditorium was built. We danced in our homes, sometimes with boys, sometimes by ourselves. There was always the radio. We listened to lots of shows-- Eddie Cantor, Jack Benny, "Hello Hollywood" and many others.

Because of the Maine blue laws*, all the movie houses were closed on Sundays, so we had to improvise. We went for walks in the afternoon and often in the evenings, too. We walked to Winslow and downtown and to the parks. We were patrons of the carnivals, the fairs, and the medicine show-- all held in Waterville. Jeannette and I walked everywhere with our arms around each other, singing, giggling, and chatting away like magpies. On hot summer afternoons, we went to the lake. Every Sunday, a truck picked people up who wished to go to the nearest lake. For fifteen cents, we could spend the afternoon on the beach. Neither of us could swim, but we enjoyed wading and romping in the water with our modest one-piece bathing suits. It was fun. We ate hotdogs and drank soda pop for lunch. For us, that was a real treat!

Jeannette and I did not always enjoy the same movies. I loved romantic musicals like "Naughty Marietta" with Jeannette MacDonald and Nelson Eddy. "Anthony Adverse", with Frederick March and Olivia de Havilland was one of my very favorite movies of all time. I also loved "Little Women" with Katherine Hepburn as Jo. I cannot tell you how many times I

---

* *"Blue laws" were laws limiting a variety of "sinful" activities. These included entertainments and the consumption of alcohol in bars and restaurants as well as its sale in stores.*

went to see that! Anything with an historical background, "Marie Antoinette" with Norma Shearer and "A Tale of Two Cities" with Ronald Coleman, I loved. Erroll Flynn and Maureen O'Hara were two of my favorite stars. And I thought Nelson Eddy was the most handsome man I had ever seen-- and I still do! My friend Jeannette preferred adventure and mystery stories. I usually ended up going to my favorite movies with Doris and Anita, my neighborhood friends. Both Doris and Anita came close to being kindred spirits to me.

I was married to Roland on September 2, 1939. Jeannette was my bridesmaid. Fifty years later, I wrote to Jeannette in Stratford, Connecticut, to ask her to attend our fiftieth anniversary as an honored guest. She never answered me. Her aunt Helen lives in Waterville. She told me that Jeannette does not remember being my bridesmaid. She said she remembers me as a friend, but she cannot place herself as having been my bridesmaid. She did not attend our anniversary celebration.

Our wedding picture hangs on our bedroom wall. In it is the whole wedding party. There, beside me, is Jeannette. She is wearing a long, blue gown with tiny bows of pink ribbons all over it. She is wearing a matching hat. I would have loved to have seen Jeannette again after all these years. I would have told her that, at one time, I thought the world of her.

Why couldn't Jeannette remember? Gloria would have.

Young Adulthood

On the heels of the Depression, and equal to it in effect, the Second World War dramatically shaped the young adulthood of the lifewriters whose stories appear in this book.

Young men who might otherwise have settled down to work on the farm or in the mill went to places they would never otherwise have ventured to, and they learned to make war. The women supported the war effort at home with defense industry jobs and then, perhaps after a hurried wedding, they followed their men to military camps.

For many families, the war brought steady work at long last, after the precarious years of the Depression.

Trudy Laliberté had the opportunity for job training she had had no hope to expect before the war (p. 127). For Bill Fagan, orphaned of his mother and cut off from his father, the war abruptly ended a newly-established family bond. ("If World War Two had not intervened, I probably would still be there today." p. 162) For Evelyn Doyon too, the war interfered with a relationship (see below).

In the stories of the war years, we learn how young adults adapted and survived. Their stories show how they used the fabric of family history and inheritance woven with the unique patterns of their own generation to fashion a life for themselves, to live out, with humor, determination and hope, their own lifestories.

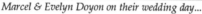

Marcel & Evelyn Doyon on their wedding day...   *and on their honeymoon-- in New York City, 1945.*

New York by Evelyn Doyon

Evelyn Fournier Doyon has raised seven children and has been both a homemaker and a hairdresser. Soleil Press editorial intern, Stephanie Doyon, who has worked many hours on this book, is her granddaughter.

It was Saturday night. Christmas was only a few weeks away. I had just finished talking on the phone with Marcel. He had been stationed at Camp Shelby since April and had not come home on leave since his two weeks in July.

In our weekly phone calls and daily letters, we planned that somehow we would spend the holidays together, but tonight all our plans were shattered.

He had received orders to go to New Jersey, the following week, to a port of embarkation and to board a ship for Europe as soon as one was available.

I was crushed. What a disappointment! He was going away to fight in the war, and we might never see each other again! We might never wear those rings tucked away in the cedar chest he had given me for my birthday! The home that we dreamed about, if it ever did materialize, seemed ages away!

Needless to say, I spent the next week waiting for Marcel's next call. This time, it came from New York City. He had gotten a week-end pass and was at the U.S.O. with his friend Ben Popadak, who was a neighbor of mine in Lisbon Falls. He and Ben were having a good time in the city. It was their first visit there and, at that time, the soldiers were made to feel welcome wherever they went.

We couldn't talk long because the phone lines were so busy, and there was always a line waiting at the pay phones. We said our goodbyes, and he promised to call again next week.

After we hung up, I got the greatest idea! New York was only a day away by train-- why not make the trip?

So I called Mrs. Doyon. She also thought it was a good idea to go down. We recruited Mrs. Popadak, Ben's mother, to come with us, too. There was only one problem-- how would we contact the boys when we arrived? But that didn't deter us. Wouldn't they be surprised!

Monday evening, after a long, tedious, and anxious ride, we three ladies, who had never traveled farther than Boston, arrived at Pennsylvania Station in New York City. We took a taxi to the Statler Hotel.

I had made a reservation through the Statler in Boston-- a hotel that hosted the Hair-dressers Convention I had attended. It was a very sensible thing to have done. As we stood in line to check in, we realized that without a reservation we would have been in real trouble.

Tuesday morning we called the Red Cross to contact the boys. We furnished them with their A.P.O. and their "dog tag" numbers, their reason for being in the city, and, of course, our telephone number at the hotel. We were sure that having given all this information, we would surely be seeing Marcel and Ben before the day was over. One of us stayed in the room waiting for that phone call at all times.

Most of our time off from phone sitting was spent in the lobby of the hotel. It was lavishly decorated with hundreds of the most beautiful poinsettias we had ever seen. The latest Christmas songs, such as Bing Crosby's "White Christmas", were being played on the sound system. All those people in the lobby, who were probably there for the same reason we were, provided our entertainment when it wasn't our turn to be by the phone.

Once in a while, I ventured outdoors and walked around the block to gaze at the tall buildings, making sure the Statler was in view. When Marcel came, we'd all go sightseeing.

For five days, this went on! As each day passed, our hopes grew dimmer and dimmer. Finally, it was Christmas Eve. We went to Midnight Mass in a little church just around the corner. Early on Christmas Day, we reluctantly boarded the train for home. You can imagine how we felt!

It was good to get back home, away from all the hustle and bustle. Maybe I would get a call from New York. Just as I sat down to relax, the phone rang. I couldn't believe my ears-- it was Marcel, at last! When I told him about our trip, he paused for a moment. He would be right home on the next plane, he said. He forged a pass and, only hours later, we went to meet him at the airport. This was really my best Christmas present ever.

We celebrated for four days. When a telegram came from his commanding officer saying he was A.W.O.L., he immediately went back to his barracks to be shipped overseas. He assured me that probably the worst thing that could happen to him was that he'd be put in the brig crossing the ocean.

That never even happened. He reported for duty the next day and not much was said about his escapade.

I will always remember that Christmas.

Appendix B: Additional Reading

Lifewriting bibliography

Blumenthal, Michael. *The New Story of Your Life.* New York, MacMillan. 1985. How-to.

Coberly, Lenore. *Writers Have No Age.* New York, The Haworth Press. 1982. Writings from senior center programs.

Daniel, Lois. *How to Write Your Own Life Story.* Chicago, Chicago Review Press. 1980.

Dixon, Janice and **Dora Flack.** *Preserving Your Past.* New York, Doubleday. 1977.

Hoffman, William. *Life Writing: A Guide to Family Journals and Personal Memoirs.* New York, St. Martin's Press. 1982.

Keen, Sam. *Telling Your Story, A Guide to Who You Are and Who You Could Be.* New York, New American Library. 1974. Very helpful for getting beyond the *what*.

Kivig, David and **Myron A. Marty.** *Your Family History: A Handbook for Research and Writing.* Arlington Heights, Illinois, Harlan Davidson, Inc. 1978.

Nichols, Evelyn and **Anne Lowenkopf.** *Lifelines, A Guide to Writing Your Personal Recollections.* Crozet, Virginia, Betterway Publications. 1989. Lists of writing topics.

Stone, Elizabeth. *Black Sheep and Kissing Cousins.* New York, MacMillan. 1988. Psychological and anthropological insights into family stories.

Thomas, Frank. *How To Write the Story of Your Life.* Cincinnati, Writer's Digest Books. 1984. Full of ideas.

Wakefield, Dan. *The Story of Your Life, Writing A Spiritual Autobiography.* Boston, Beacon Press. 1990. Less hands-on and more into the *why*.

Weitzman, David. *My Backyard History Book.* Boston, Little, Brown and Company. 1975. Geared to children; full of good info.

Booklist of autobiographies and memoirs

Adams, Henry. *The Education of Henry Adams.* Grandson of John Q. Adams.

Angelou, Maya. *I Know Why the Caged Bird Sings* .

Antin, Mary. *The Promised Land.* An immigrant girl's story.

Arlen, Michael. *Passage to Ararat.* A search for Armenian roots.

Baker, Russell. *Growing Up.* A story of the author's early Depression years.

Beston, Henry. *Northern Farm,* and *Outermost House.* Journals of a naturalist.

Bourke-White, Margaret. *Portrait of Myself.* Magazine photojournalist.

Brittain, Vera. *Testament of Youth.* World War I nurse.

Burns, George. *Living it up.* Comedian.

Cahan, Abraham. *The Education of Abraham Cahan.* Immigrant Jewish newspaper editor.

Campanella, Roy. *It's Good to Be Alive.* Baseball player.

Chao, Buwei Yang. *Autobiography of a Chinese Woman.* Chinese in America.

Chaplin, Charlie. *My Autobiography.*

Chernin, Kim. *In My Mother's House.* Growing up in a Communist home in the 40s and 50s.

Conway, Jill Ker. *The Road from Coorain.* From Australian poverty to college presidency.

Dinesen, Isak. *Out of Africa.* Danish woman in Kenya.

Dilliard, Annie. *An American Childhood.*

Douglass, Frederick. *Narrative of the Life of Frederick Douglass.* 19th c. African-American.

Durant, Will and **Ariel.** *A Dual Autobiography.* Historians and philosophers.

Ford, Betty. *The Times of My Life.*

Frank, Anne. *The Diary of a Young Girl.* Jewish girl in hiding in World War II.

Gandhi, Mohandas K. *Autobiography.*

Gilbreth, Frank and **Carey,** and **Ernestine Gilbreth.** *Cheaper by the Dozen.*

Greene, Graham. *A Sort of Life.* **Novelist.**

Haley, Alex. *Roots.* Dramatic novelization of the author's family stories.

Hall, Donald. *String Too Short to Be Saved.* Stories about the author's Yankee grandparents.

Hall, Edward. *An Anthropology of Everyday Life.* Anthropologist looks at his life.

Hayes, Helen. *On Reflection, An Autobiography.* "Grande Dame" of the American theater.

Hemingway, Ernest. *A Moveable Feast.* The artist's life in Paris in the 20s and 30s.

Herriot, James. *All Things Bright and Beautiful.* English veterinarian between the wars.

Keller, Helen. *Story of My Life.*

Jung, Carl. *Memories, Dreams, and Reflections.*

Kerouac, Jack. *Lonesome Traveller.* Beat generation spokesman.

Kingston, Maxine Hong. *The Woman Warrior: Memoirs of a Girlhood Among Ghosts.*

Lewis, C.S. *Surprised by Joy: The Shape of My Early Life.* Novelist.

Linkletter, Art. *I Didn't Do it Alone.* TV personality.

McCarthy, Mary. *Memories of A Catholic Girlhood.* Novelist.

Meir, Golda. *My Life.* Israeli politician.

Nin, Anaïs. *Diaries.* Literary and psychological memoirs in several volumes.

Neruda, Pablo. *Memoirs.* Literary and political autobiography of the Chilean Nobel laureate.

Rodriguez, Richard. *Hunger of Memory.* Hispanic-American tells of early years.

Sarton, May. *The House by the Sea, At Seventy,* and *After the Stroke.* Journals.

Schultz, J. W. *My Life as an Indian.* Late 19th c. account of life with the Blackfoot Indians.

Sills, Beverly. *Bubbles.* Soprano.

Stein, Gertrude. *The Autobiography of Alice B. Toklas.* A memoir of Paris literary life.

Roosevelt, Eleanor. *On My Own.*

Roth, Philip. *Patrimony.* A son's experience of his father's death by cancer.

Washington, Booker. *Up From Slavery.*

Welty, Eudora. *One Writer's Beginnings.* Welty's development as a writer.

Wilder, Laura Ingalls. *On the Way Home.* American frontier stories.

Wong, Jade Snow. *Fifth Chinese Daughter.* Growing up Chinese American.

Zweig, Paul. *Departures.* Sexual autobiography and journal of the author's dying of cancer.

Writing-- technique, motivation & promotion

Brande, Dorothea. *Becoming a Writer.* New York, Harcourt, Brace. 1934.

Duncan, Lois. *How to Write and Sell Your Personal Experiences.* Cincinnati, Writer's Digest Books. 1982. Especially for those who want to be "real" writers.

Goldberg, Natalie. *Writing Down The Bones.* Boston, Shambala Press. 1986. Good for exploring your feelings about being a person who is writing.

Kremer, John. 101 Ways to Market Your Books. Fairfield, Iowa, Ad-Lib Publications. 1986.

Poynter, Dan. *The Self-Publishing Manual: How To Write, Print, and Sell Your Own Book.* Santa Barbara, California, Para Publishing. 1986. Excellent guide to self-publishing.

Rico, Gabriele Lusser. *Writing the Natural Way: Using Right-Brain Techniques to Release Your Expressive Powers.* Los Angeles, J.P. Tarcher, Inc. 1983. A hands-on book.

Strunk, William and **E.B. White.** *The Elements of Style.* New York, Macmillan. 1972. An excellent resource on grammar and style.

Zinsser, Wiliam. *On Writing Well.* New York, Harper and Row. 1989.

Visualization & self-growth

Adair, Margo. *Working Inside Out, Tools for Change: Applied Meditation for Intuitive Problem Solving.* Berkeley, Wingbow Books. 1984

Campbell, Joseph. *The Hero with a Thousand Faces.* Princeton, Princeton Universty Press. 1949. Studies the universality of myths from around the world.
The Masks of God. Vol. 1-4. New York, Viking. 1959-1968. Myths examined across the ages and cultures. An important series.

Gawain, Shakti. *Creative Visualization* and *Living in the Light.* San Rafael, Cal., Whatever Publishing. 1978,1986. Text with excercises and affirmations. Very accessible.

Jung, Carl. *Symbols of Transformation.* Princeton, Princeton University Press. 1967. Everday symbols from many cultures. Helpful in understanding personal symbols.

Larsen, Stephen. *The Mythic Imagination.* New York, Bantam Books. 1990. Helpful in understanding our personal myths and using them for tools of change.

Levinson, Daniel. *The Seasons of a Man's Life.* New York, Knopf. 1978. Men's life stages.

Pearson, Carol. *The Hero Within/ Six Archetypes We Live By.* New York, Harper Row. 1986. Everyday archetypes. Full of exercises for understanding archetypes in our lives.

Schaef, Anne Wilson. *Women's Reality.* Minn., Minn., Winston Press. 1981. Women's culture and life development.

Index

also from
Soleil ✳ Press

Turning Memories: An Audio Guide to Writing Lifestories $16.95
The heart of *Turning Memories Into Memoirs* read by the author in a 120-minute, two-tape set. Handy for those who enjoy making the most of driving time or chores that leave the mind free. A great refresher to get you back to work on your lifestories.

The Photo Scribe: A Writing Guide
How to Write the Stories Behind Your Photographs $16.95
Ever wish you could write the story the photo didn't catch? This book is for you. A step-by-step photo-journaling guide with exercises, examples, instructions. Its friendly tone details how you can write short meaningful narratives to expand on photos in your albums and memory books. 40+ contemporary and period photos, sample narratives. Endorsed by Creative Memories co-founder Rhonda Anderson.

Memory Binders   each/$21.95
The Lifewriter's Memory Binder
The Photoscribe's Memory Binder
The Genealogist's Memory Binder
The Memory Binders are customized 80-page workbooks with exercises, worksheets, and instruction to complement and supplement our titles. Each binder contains photo and artifact pockets, indexed sections for exercises, worksheets, and notes. Think of these are versatile workshop and handbook organizers and extenders.

Mail-a-Memory™ **Memory Gathering Stationery**
Boxed Note Card Sets   6 sets, boxed/$12.95
A lovely stationery set and a handy tool to gather memories and stories from distant friends and relatives. 3-piece set includes envelope, note card, and 2-fold return self-mailer. Designed to fit your photo-safe albums.
Post Cards   one dozen/$9.95
5" x 7" cards with evocative pen-and-ink drawings and ample space to record a memory. Perfect for on-the-spot memory making at receptions, showers, reunions.

Ordering Information
Call for **shipping rates** or visit *www.turningmemories.com/ordrform.html*
For **VISA/MC** orders, call toll free, **1-888-80-STORY**, 9 AM- 5 PM, EST.
E-mail your VISA/MC order to **memoirs@turningmemories.com**.
Write to us : 95 Gould Road #12, Lisbon Falls, ME 04252.

✳ ✳ ✳ ✳ ✳

Are you a teacher or workshop presenter?
Is your club or community organization planning a fundraiser?
Our popular memory-preserving materials make great back-of-the-room sales items for classes and fundraisers. Significant volume discounts apply when orders are shipped to one address. Please inquire about this meaningful—and simple—way to raise income by providing quality books and tapes to lifestory writers in your community.

Should you be leading
Turning Memories workshops?

The Soleil Lifestory Network

The **Soleil Lifestory Network** is an international affiliation of dedicated lifewriting professionals experienced in assisting people in the writing of their personal and family stories. Our seminar leaders facilitate workshops, seminars, and programs using the **Turning Memories™** method, curriculum, and materials.

If you have a writing and/or teaching background, becoming a **Turning Memories** workshop presenter could be an stimulating next step in your professional development. As an independent **Soleil Lifestory Network Affiliate**, you can earn full or part-time income doing creative work that's truly significant—for you and for your community. Inquire today!

Network Support from the Main Office

Affiliates receive these on-going business and vocational supports:
- the **Presenter's and Curriculum Manuals**, the only comprehensive how-to guides to launch and sustain your workshop delivery business.
- the **Publicity Template Disk** of posters & press releases to jumpstart your outreach.
- **profitable discounts** on a growing library of lifewriting support materials— including all our books, audio guides, workbooks and binders.
- **unlimited phone consultation** with & **guidance** from the main office to facilitate your on-going work. You work **for** yourself, **not by** yourself.
- helpful **client referrals** from the main office to fill your workshops.
- a **professional listing** on our World Wide Web Site.
- **complimentary copies** of all new lifewriting titles.

The Most Important Step You'll Ever Take

is always the next step! So step into the
Soleil Lifestory Network
Call today: 1-207-353-5454.
You have nothing to lose and so much to gain!

✳ ✳ ✳ ✳ ✳

Lifestory writers—

Are you struggling alone with writing your stories?
Could working with a writing coach put you over the top?
Inquire about our Soleil Editing Services. We'll work with you to bring your memoir or memorial project to a successful completion.

✳

Sponsor a workshop in your town

For details, contact us at **workshops@turningmemories.com** or write 95-12 Gould Rd., Lisbon Falls, ME 04252. Ask about **Affiliate** workshops near you, too.